Using Cr

Read *Using Creati*[illegible]*chniques* and learn how to—

- See the world around you from a new and fresh perspective.
- Expand your use of your camera and its controls.
- Mix and match accessories and films to create exciting new images.
- Create your own reality by combining individual images in one photograph.

THE NO NONSENSE LIBRARY

OTHER NO NONSENSE PHOTOGRAPHY GUIDES

Composing Photographs
Photographing People
Photographing Your Vacation
Using Accessory Equipment
Using Existing Light

OTHER NO NONSENSE GUIDES

Car Guides
Career Guides
Cooking Guides
Financial Guides
Health Guides
Legal Guides
Parenting Guides
Real Estate Guides
Study Guides
Success Guides
Wine Guides

NO NONSENSE PHOTOGRAPHY GUIDE™

USING CREATIVE TECHNIQUES

A KODAK Book

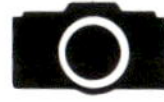

ROBERT HERKO

Longmeadow Press

USING CREATIVE TECHNIQUES

Published by Longmeadow Press, 201 High Ridge Road, Stamford, Connecticut 06904.

ISBN 0-681-40729-8

Produced by The Image Bank in association with
Eastman Kodak Company, Rochester, New York.

Printed in Spain

0 9 8 7 6 5 4 3 2 1

Producer: Solomon M. Skolnick; *Managing Editor:* Elizabeth Loonan; *Editors:* Terri Hardin (The Image Bank), Margaret Buckley (Kodak); *Production Director:* Charles W. Styles (Kodak); *Production Coordinator:* Ann-Louise Lipman (The Image Bank); *Editorial Assistant:* Carol Raguso; *Production Assistant:* Valerie Zars; *Photo Researchers:* Natalie Goldstein, Lenore Weber; *Copy Editor:* Irene S. Korn; *Art Direction and Design:* Chase/Temkin & Associates, Inc.

Cover photographs, left to right: Bill Carter, Al Satterwhite, Melchior DiGiacomo

For information about the photographs in this book, please contact:
The Image Bank
111 Fifth Avenue
New York, NY 10003

TABLE OF CONTENTS

INTRODUCTION

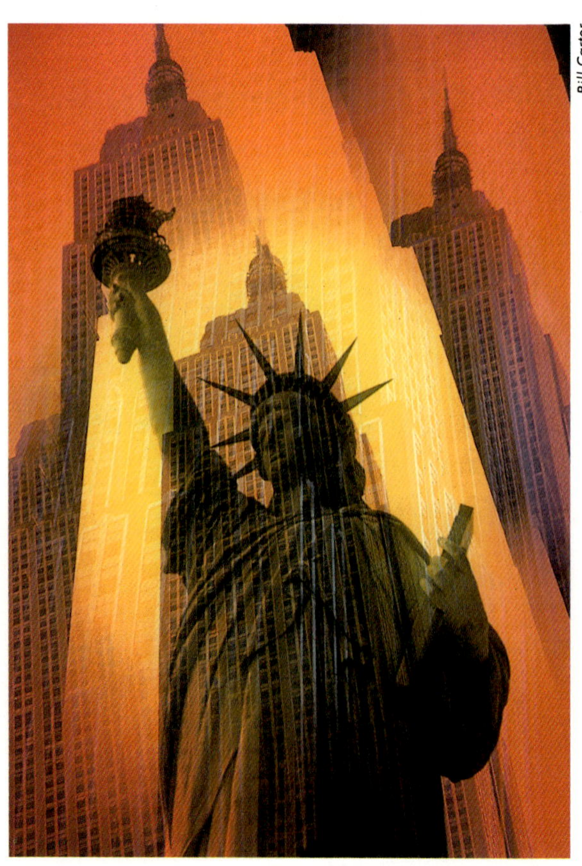
Bill Carter

Being creative in your photography can be as easy as moving your camera at the same time you take a picture. Other techniques may not be quite as simple as this, and a few may require accessory equipment, but by combining the techniques you will learn here and your own imagination, you'll discover the rewards of exercising your creativity in new ways.

You may already be applying such creative techniques as backlighting or varying your viewpoint and camera angle. This book will expand your creative applications of photography through the use of unusual filters, selective focus, panning the camera, exposure techniques to achieve special effects, and pushing film to enhance grain.

If you want to expand your photographic horizons, these techniques may mean the difference between just taking a picture and "painting" with your camera.

Using Creative Techniques can show you how to get started on the road to more creative photographs. It will show you how to experiment with your camera controls and the wide variety of films that are available today. By understanding the contributions of film itself, you can learn a lot about how your images will appear. This book will show you how to "warm up" creatively to get in the right mood to explore photography in ways you hadn't thought of before. And it will discuss accessory equipment such as filters and lenses as they apply to more unusual and creative photography.

Look closely at the photographs in this book. Which ones do you like best? How were they made? Now look at photographs you have taken. Can you identify one that you could have improved by applying a creative technique?

Read through the book carefully to see which techniques appeal to you. If you come across a word you don't understand, check the glossary of terms at the back of the book.

Then take your camera, experiment, and check the results. Don't be afraid to make mistakes. Your experiences will help strengthen your visual perception and give you more creative control over your pictures.

PART ONE 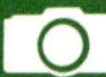

YOUR CREATIVE WARM-UP

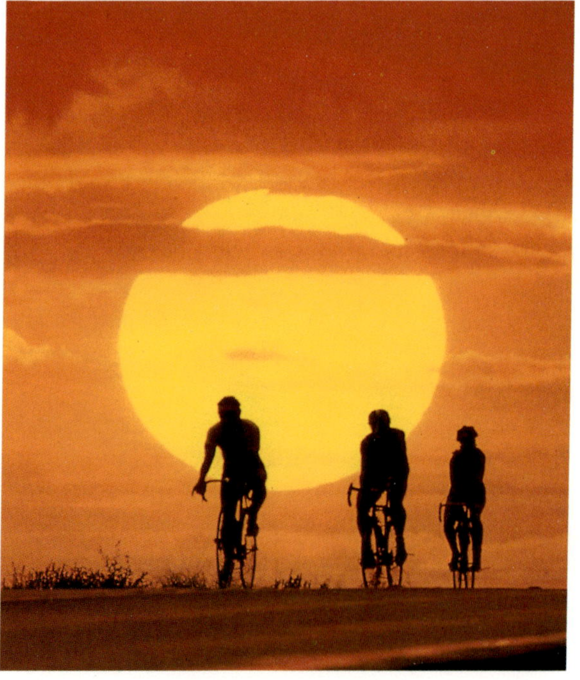

Kaz Mori

To learn how to use creative techniques effectively, first "warm up" to the process of experimenting with your camera. Read your camera manual from cover to cover to learn about features of your camera that you may not have used before. By learning more about and being able to use all the capabilities of your camera, you will grow more comfortable with it. This will relax you and set the stage for more creative control.

Second, take out your photograph album and review the pictures you've taken in the past. What are your photographic strong points: composition, lighting, capturing the moment? What are your weak points? What do you perceive as *your* style? Employing creative techniques may not give you the exciting images you want if you don't know where to begin.

Next, look around you and try to see things as if you were seeing them for the very first time. Do you see the shapes and colors of shadows? When Gauguin painted a shadow, for example, he gave it a shape and color all its own. How about the reflections of shapes and colors on water? How many ways could they be captured?

In Part One, we will discuss the impact of changing your perspective, as well as tilting the frame, photographing mirrors and reflections, collaging and coloring prints, and cropping images. Although these aren't "creative techniques" in themselves, they will get you used to looking at subjects and thinking about photography in a creative way.

CHANGING YOUR POINT OF VIEW

The level from which you shoot a photograph is your *viewpoint* or *point of view*. If, for instance, you stand at the base of the John Hancock Building in Chicago (or the Empire State Building in New York City) and take a picture of it, the building looks tall and imposing. Your point of view would be called the *ant's- (*or *worm's-) eye view*. If you go to the observation deck of either building and take a picture looking down on the city, your point of view would be a *bird's-eye view*.

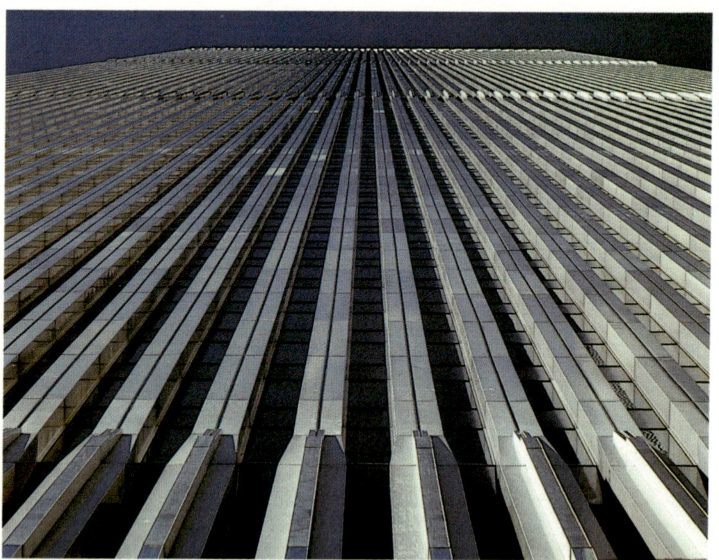

Don Landwehrle

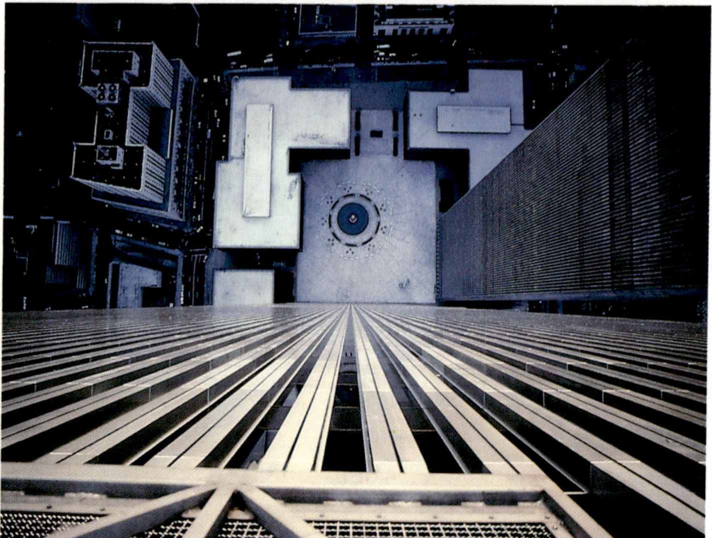

Steve Krongard

A photograph taken from an ant's- (or worm's-) eye view distorts the subject, making it appear imposing and monumental; a bird's-eye view of the same subject carries the viewer to dizzying heights.

An ant's-eye view gives an interesting perspective to this friendly game.

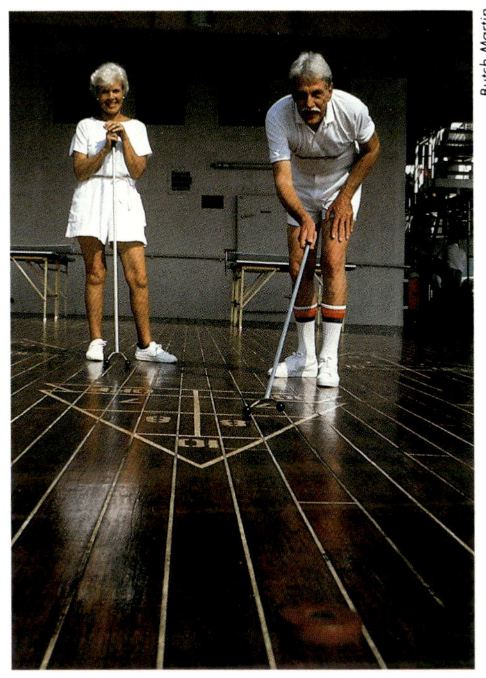

Butch Martin

These are only two examples of the many points of view from which you can take pictures. People often forget that creativity in photography begins with how you record what you see. Often you automatically take photos at your own eye level to relate to your subjects. For example, when you make a full-length photograph of a person, you tend to stand upright with the camera at eye level. And when you're shooting subjects up close, it's hard to get the entire person in the vertical frame of the viewfinder unless you tilt the camera at a slight angle, either upwards or downwards, depending on your own height.

If you tilt your camera up or down, you are not going to get an accurate view of your subject. When you look down, your subject is diminished and perspective is reduced or foreshortened. Looking up extends perspective, making objects and people appear larger and taller. Neither way represents your subject's true scale.

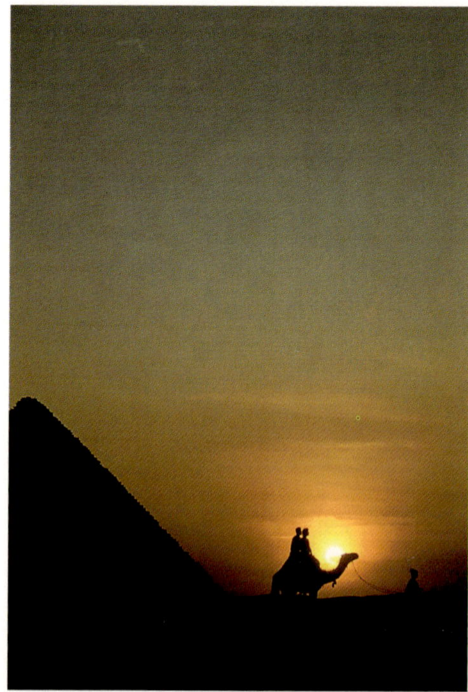

Brett Froomer

Your point of view also depends on your distance from the subject. In the picture at the left, a long shot relates the subject to the environment; in the photograph below, a closer shot emphasizes the subject.

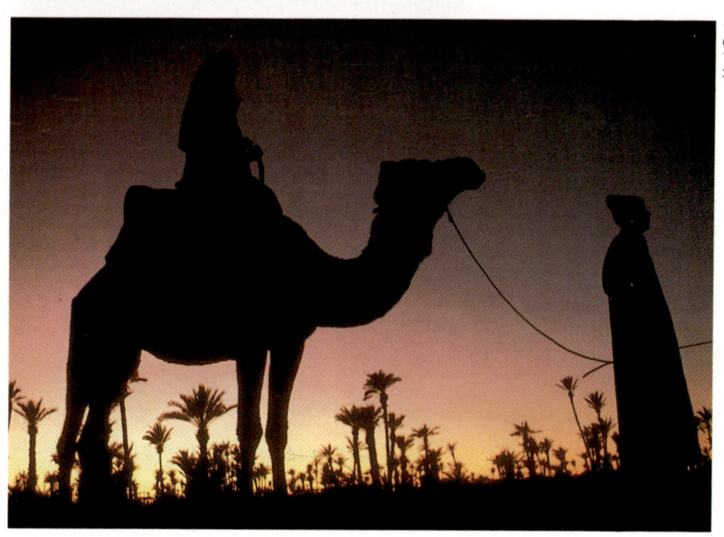

Yuri Dojc

But no law says that you must take all pictures by standing upright and holding a camera at eye level just because you are accustomed to seeing objects and people from that height. The next time you take a picture, try centering the person's waist in the viewfinder; then, if you still can't get your subject entirely in the picture, back away until you do. You'll find that your subject looks more proportionate and realistic.

Next, try assuming the viewpoint of a child, a pet, or a very tall basketball player. Break the monotony of the eye-level viewpoint by photographing your subject every which way. Try profiles and back views. Get up on a ladder and photograph the top of your subject's head!

Experiment with variations in camera-to-subject distance by making long shots and close-ups. Most snapshots are taken at medium distances—neither very far from nor close to the subject. Why not make a series of shots, first standing far away, then as close to your subject as you can? You'll probably discover that the range at which you can take good photographs is much wider than you imagined.

Thinking in these terms helps stretch your creative instincts and prepare you for the creative techniques to come.

TILTING THE FRAME

The object of tilting the frame so that it's not parallel to the ground is the same as changing your viewpoint: it adds variety to your photographs, and helps you break the habits that keep you from developing a fresh, creative attitude.

When we make a picture, we often align the sides of the frame with the vertical or horizontal elements of the scene so that the image is squared within the frame. While diminishing the unexpected allows the viewer's eye to be drawn unencumbered to the main subject of the photo, it is not always necessary or desirable.

An off-square alignment can sometimes add to the visual impact of a photograph. When you tilt the frame, you turn both horizontal and vertical lines into diagonal ones. Diagonal lines

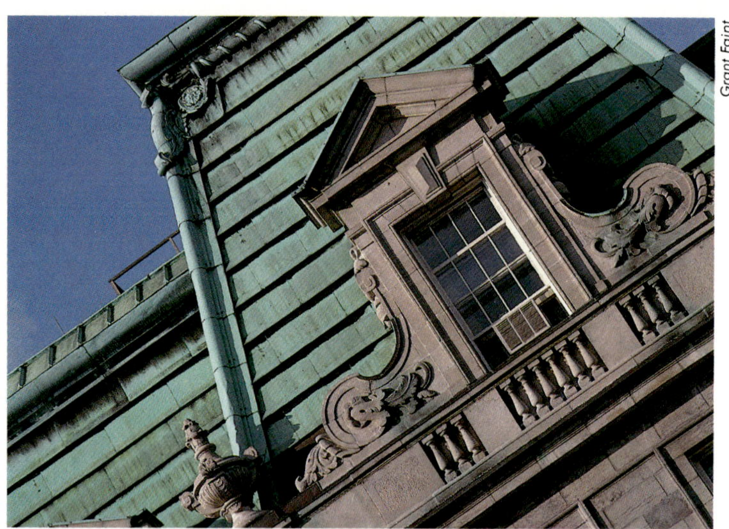

Grant Faint

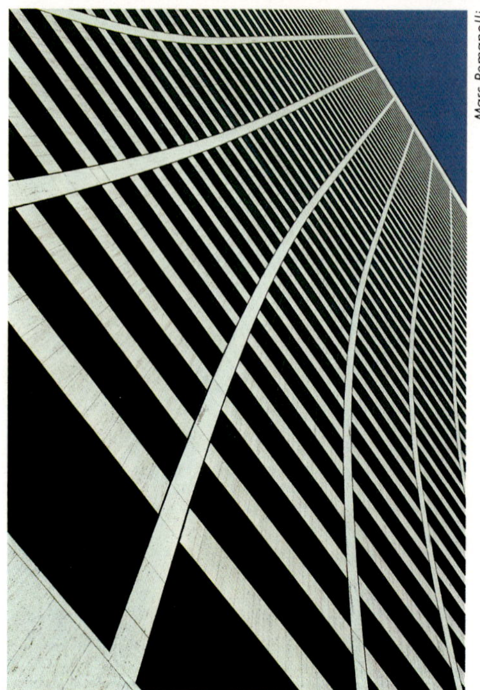

Marc Romanelli

Tilting the frame, as in the photograph at the top, can give a fresh perspective to an old subject. Tilting the frame in the photograph at the left emphasizes the distinct curve and height of the building.

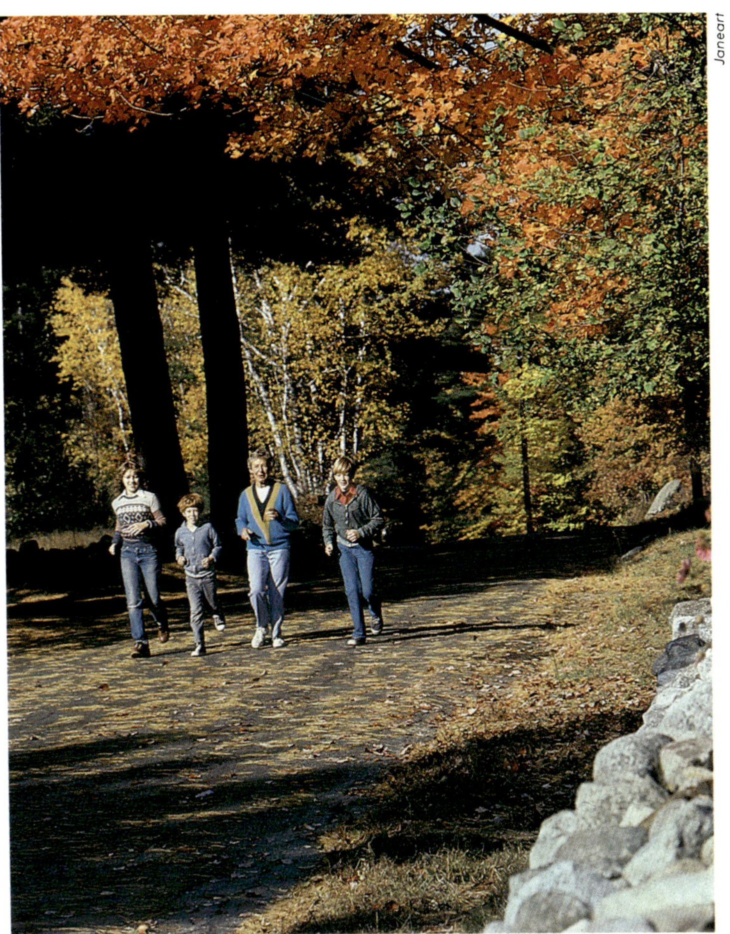
Janeart

Tilts and slants occur naturally, and can be used to add interest to the composition of your photograph.

are restless and impart much more of a sense of motion than other lines. Even if your subject is just sitting in a chair or standing, tilting the frame lends dynamics to the image.

When you tilt the frame, make sure it looks deliberate! Tilting only a little will look sloppy. You want to convey a sense of your style, not careless composition.

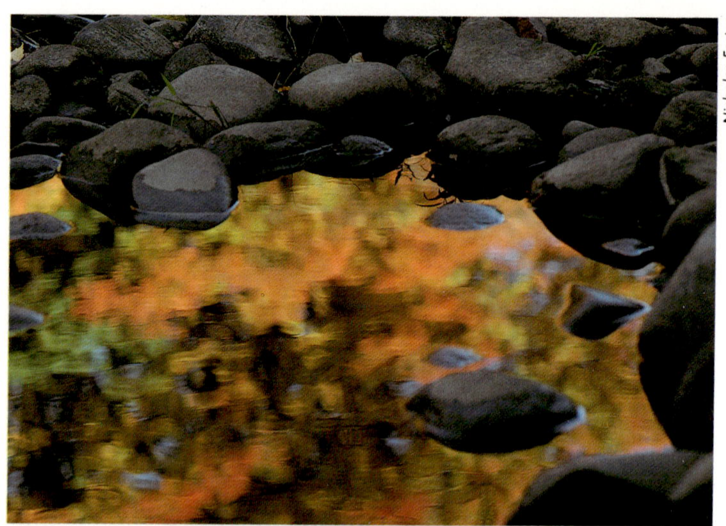

Nicholas Foster

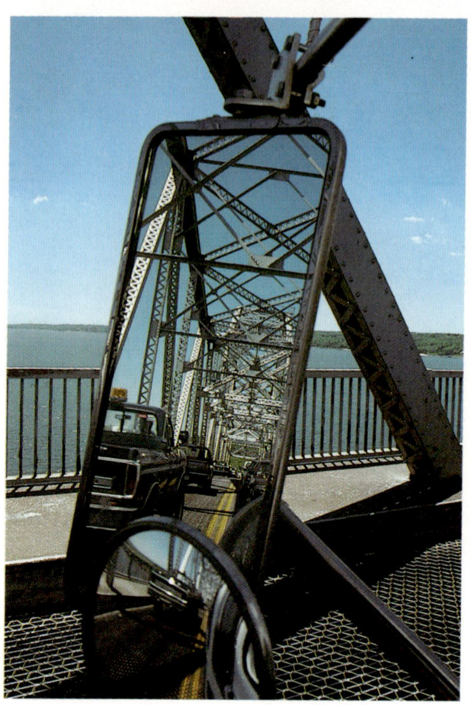

Sobel/Klonsky

Photographs of reflections may make us question what we are seeing. Reflections in nature, as in the photograph above, often evoke a contemplative mood; the photograph at the left offers a wry comment on modern society.

MIRRORS AND REFLECTIONS

Try using true or distorted reflections as additions to images or as entire images in themselves. You can usually obtain a true reflection only by photographing a flat mirrored surface, such as a mirror, a store window, or a calm puddle or pond. All other surfaces can distort the reflected image by adding color, exaggerating perspective, or adding surface imperfections. Although any shiny surface can produce distorted reflections, you can usually find the best reflections on dark or wet objects with a neutral color, such as black or grey.

You can superimpose a partially reflected (or "ghost") image on an actual scene by photographing through window glass or a similar surface. When you make such superimposed images, check the depth of field by using the preview button on your camera to be sure that both the reflection and the scene beyond will be in focus.

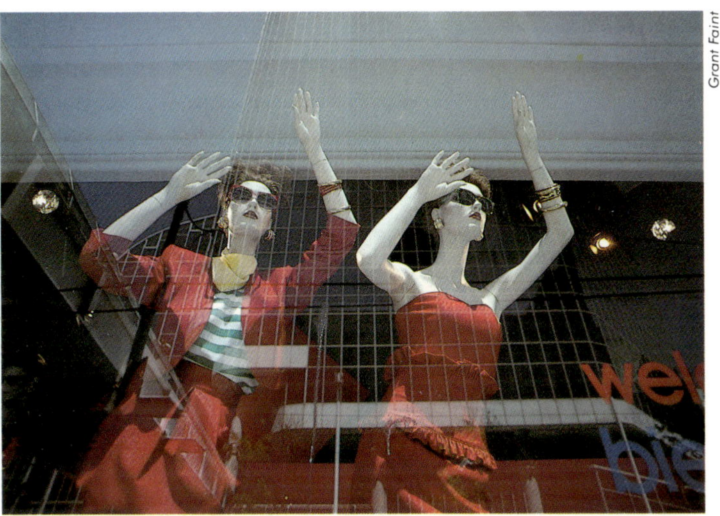

Grant Faint

Mannequins are a favorite subject because they serve as stand-ins for people and they hold their poses! In this photograph, the play between the mannequins and the reflections conveys the image of a sophisticated city.

If you use a reflection alone as your subject, consider these important points:

WHEN PHOTOGRAPHING REFLECTIONS

- Be aware of the amount of visual distortion that the reflecting surface introduces, and be sure it's acceptable to you.
- Remember that the reflective surface may produce extreme alterations in colors and tones.

To set up a simple reflection, have your subject hold a mirror so that it reflects part of his or her face. Study the most interesting angles. Remember to keep yourself out of the reflection. Stand at an angle where you can't see your own reflection through the viewfinder.

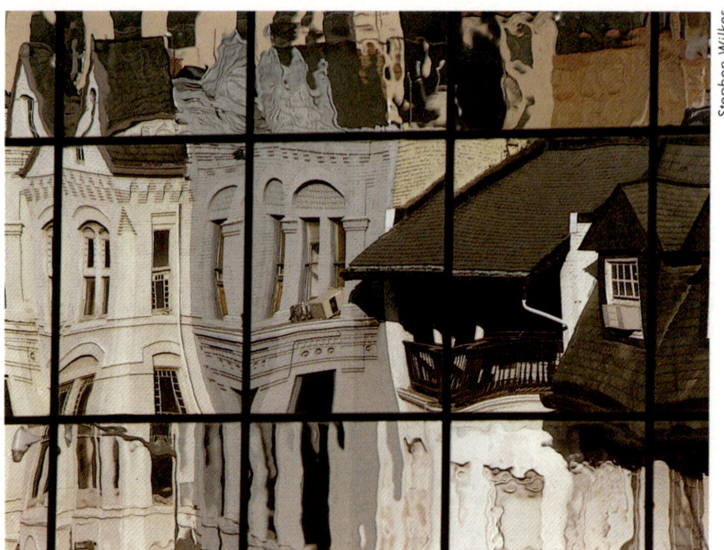

Stephen Wilkes

Town houses reflected in the mirrored glass of a modern building contrast the past and the present.

COLORING PRINTS

You can retouch almost all photographic prints by hand. While the techniques for black-and-white and color retouching are quite similar, some of the materials are different. You can hand-color black-and-white prints with several types of materials to simulate a painting or a color print. The colors will usually appear more pastel than those in a color print.

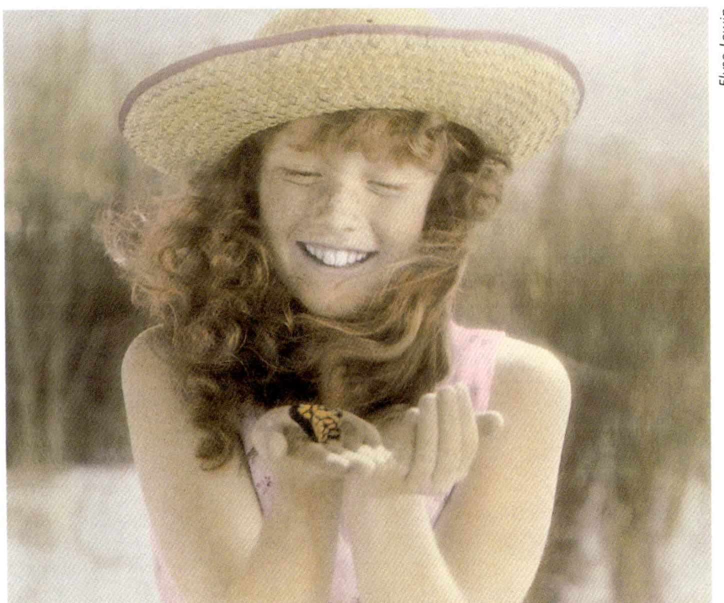

Elyse Lewin

Hand coloring is reminiscent of photography's beginnings, and is often used to evoke old-fashioned appeal.

You can use several basic types of materials to retouch prints: oil colors that remain on the surface of the print, liquid color dyes that actually penetrate the surface of the print, dry dyes that you set with steam, black graphite, colored pencils, and pastel chalks. You may find that matt-surface prints are easier to retouch than glossy prints, because the materials don't change the surface appearance. However, when you use liquid dyes that

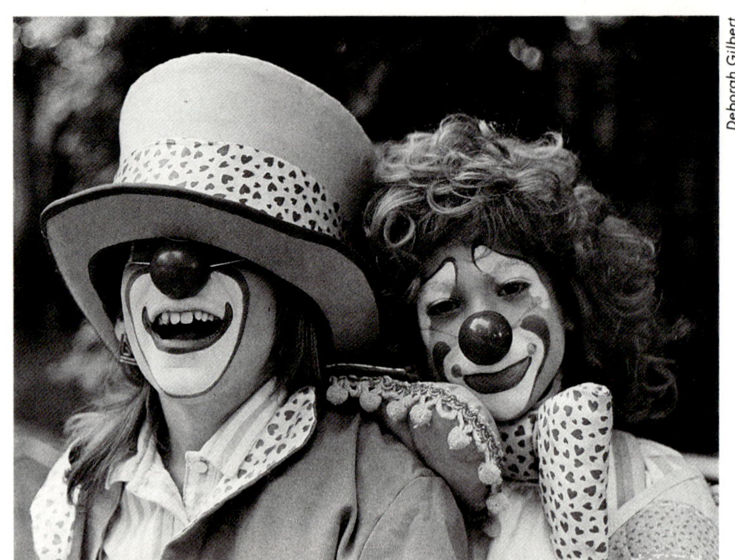

Deborah Gilbert

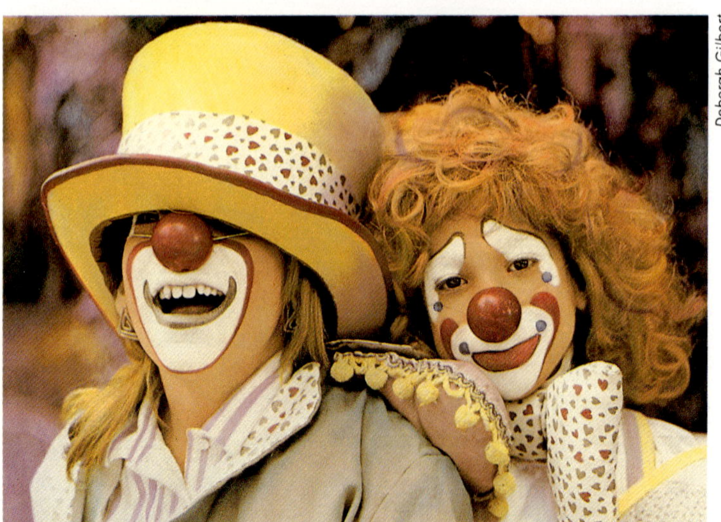

Deborah Gilbert

Hand coloring adds a new dimension to your black-and-white photographs without making them appear completely life-like. There's no need to strive for realism; going out of bounds emphasizes more graphic aspects.

penetrate the gelatin overcoat of a glossy print, the gloss is restored when the dyes dry. And when you steam-set dry dyes, the surface gloss is restored. Before using pencils, oil colors, or pastels, you must apply a retouching lacquer to make the print surface receptive to these materials.

When you hand-color black-and-white prints, you can either try to duplicate the colors of a scene or produce a completely unrealistic effect by using abstract colors—the choice is strictly up to you.

CROPPING YOUR PICTURES

Have you ever looked at your prints or slides and found them disappointing—except for a little something in the corner? By making *crop marks* on your slide mount or print, you can have your photofinisher blow up just a part of your picture to whatever size you want.

Although you should always strive for good picture quality and overall composition when you expose your photographs, cropping can be exciting and creative. And by examining your photographs closely for "croppable" elements, you may enhance what you already know about photo composition.

Cropping is used extensively in publishing. Contrary to what you may think, magazines and books do not ordinarily use the entire image when they print a photograph. A small detail isolated from a larger image may have its own distinct aesthetic value. A single photograph can provide many individual images.

Think of each photograph as a collection of photographs, and examine each one closely to discover the images within it. For example, you may photograph a subject with his or her arms akimbo, and discover that one arm artfully frames an element in the background. Or the folds of a woman's dress can become an exciting abstract image.

To indicate a crop, use horizontal or vertical lines (or both). Labs will use these lines as guides when they enlarge the image to fill a standard format.

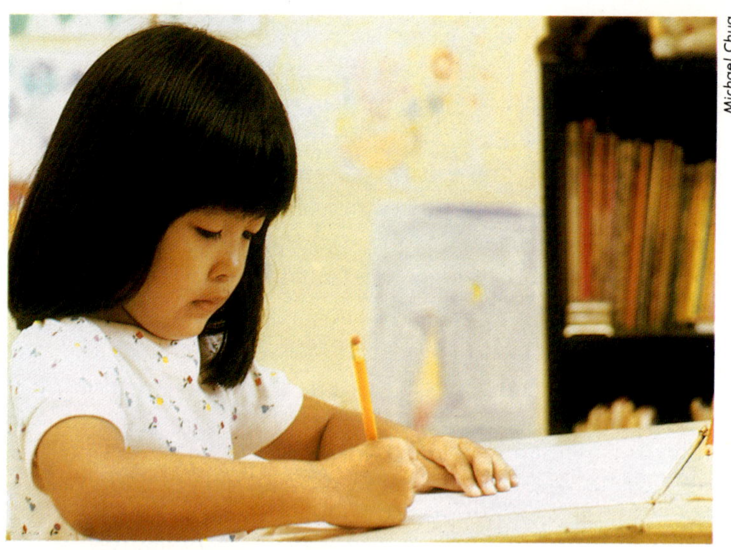

Michael Chua

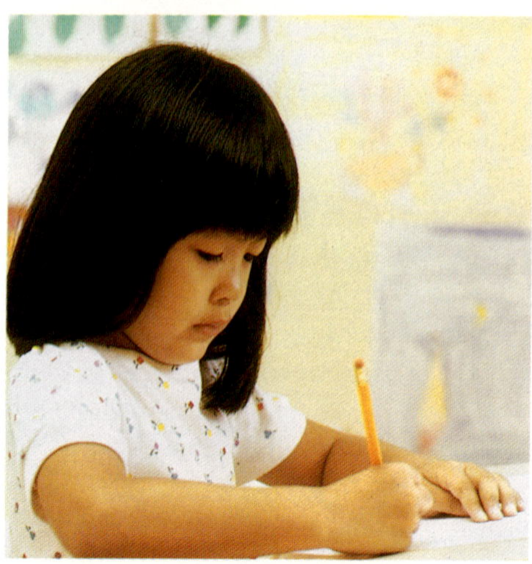

Michael Chua

Cropping out distracting objects in the background can also redefine your photograph. Here, a horizontal shot has been cropped to eliminate the dark bookshelf in the background.

When you enlarge a very small part of your photograph, you must consider the degree of enlargement and the quality you need in the enlargement. Prints from greatly enlarged negatives or slides—particularly those made on high-speed films—will have a "grainy" appearance. Graininess is usually undesirable,

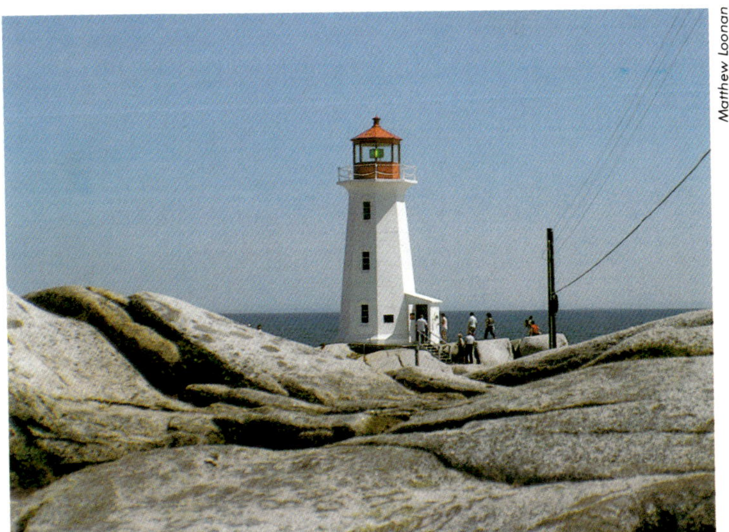

Matthew Loonan

The photograph above seems well composed, except for the telephone wires. Cropping can eliminate distracting elements.

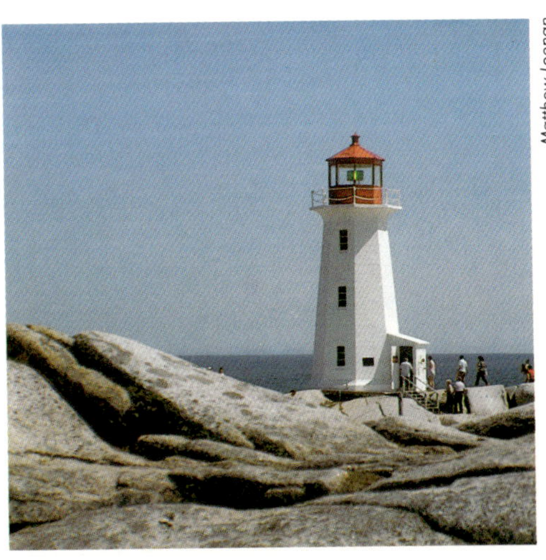

Matthew Loonan

but sometimes it can be quite attractive if you use it to produce special effects (see *enlarged grain*, page 72). To avoid graininess in big enlargements, use a film with extremely fine or micro-fine grain, such as KODAK EKTAR 25 Film. When you select your film, keep in mind the effect you are striving for.

COLLAGING PRINTS

Making a collage of prints requires only a smattering of manual skills and a few simple tools: a sharp, razor-type hobby knife (or a single-edged razor blade) or some sharp scissors, paste or photo cement, such as KODAK Rapid Mounting Cement, and some fine sandpaper for smoothing the edges of the cut materials.

Start by cutting some photographs out of a magazine. Use a large black-and-white or color print as your background; then add some visual elements cut from other photographs, magazines, etc.

Set limits that will challenge your creative instincts, such as choosing photographs of a certain tone or subject. Try combining non-photographic elements with photographic images—use anything that comes to mind, such as lace or origami paper. You can blend in the edges smoothly, or leave them rough and visible.

After assembling the collage, mount it on a wall and arrange the lighting so that it doesn't cause reflections on the surface of the collage. Look through your camera viewfinder and move in close to fill the frame with your handiwork. Placing the camera on a tripod will help you to frame accurately and avoid camera movement. Then photograph the collage with color-slide or print film.

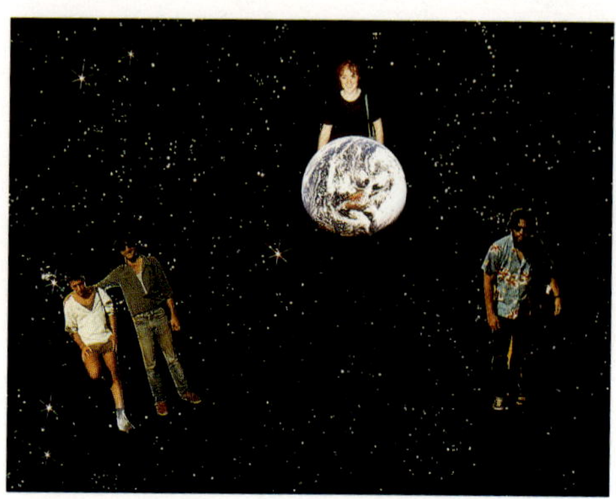

David J. Carol

Collaging calls for creative decision-making. You can be playful, as in the collage at the left.

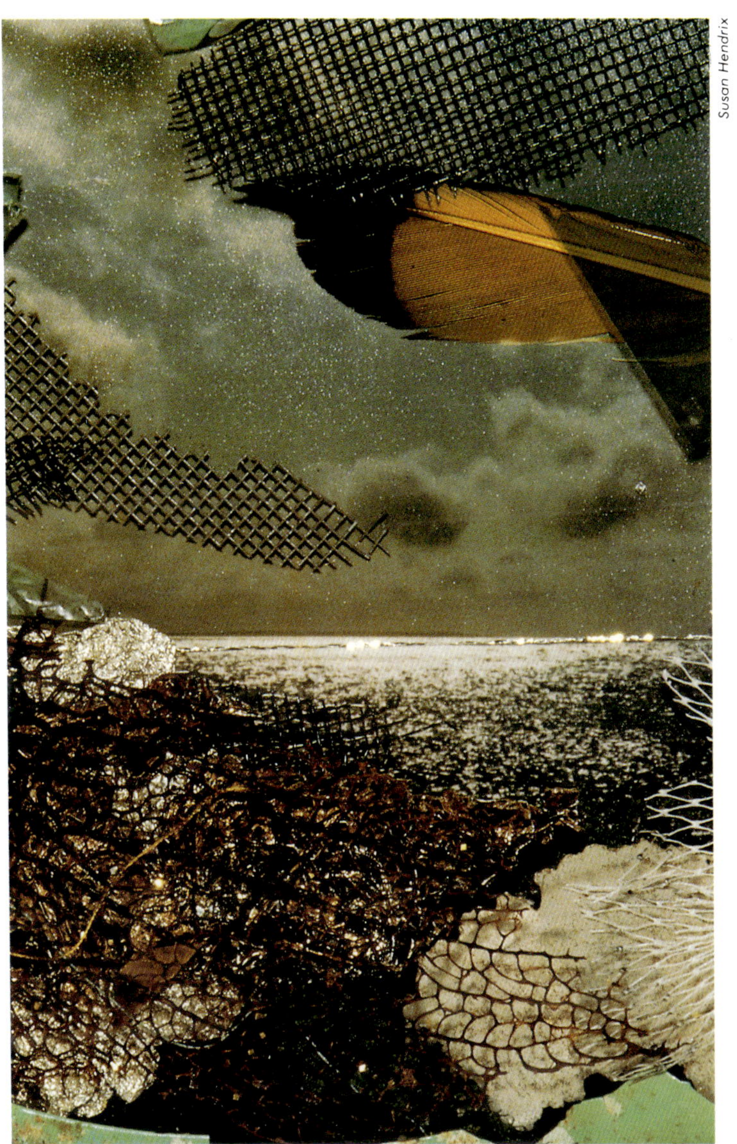

Susan Hendrix

In collaging, you can also incorporate media other than photographic images to introduce texture.

PART TWO 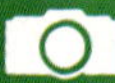

CREATIVE TECHNIQUES WITH YOUR CAMERA

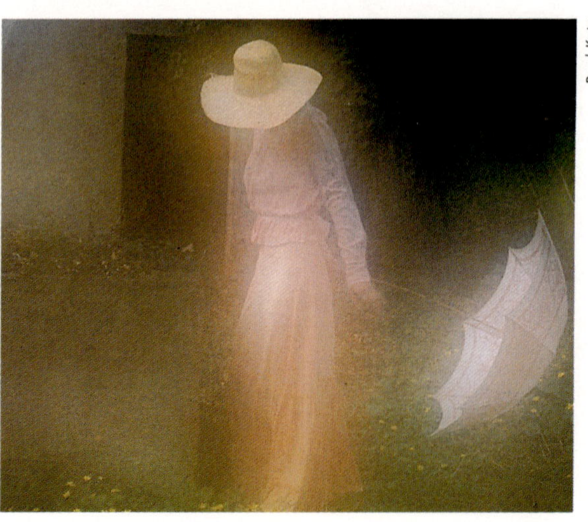

Paul Katz

After you have experimented with your camera and several types of film, you are ready for the more advanced and sophisticated techniques that will challenge your reflexes, your expertise, and your imagination.

In Part Two, we will discuss filters and selective focus; techniques for intentional blur, such as panning the camera and zooming a lens during exposure; and ideas for using exposure creatively, such as multiple and night exposures, as well as intentional overexposure.

FILTERS

One of the easiest creative techniques the beginner can tackle is producing special effects with filters. Filters are relatively inexpensive and easy to use: by simply attaching them to your camera lens, you can achieve spectacular effects.

You will probably be using a screw-mount type of filter. These filters screw directly onto your camera lens barrel. Select filters that have the same diameter as the lens you are using. If you feel unsure about selecting filters, ask your photo dealer for help.

You can buy single filters to attach to your lens individually or a comprehensive system with a holder that allows you to use a number of filters at the same time. You can even make your own special-effects filters.

If you own a lot of lenses, you may want to use an adapter ring instead of buying a filter for each lens. To avoid *vignetting*—cutting off the edges of the image—avoid using a filter with a diameter that's smaller than that of your lens.

In addition to basic filters, such as UV or skylight filters, you can purchase many other types of filters (or lens attachments) that add colors, rainbows, stars, multiple images, etc. Some filters even create an impression of movement in photos of stationary subjects. In this section, we will discuss diffusion, polarizing, single-color and dual-color, graduated, star, diffraction, and multiple-image filters, and tell you how to make your own filters.

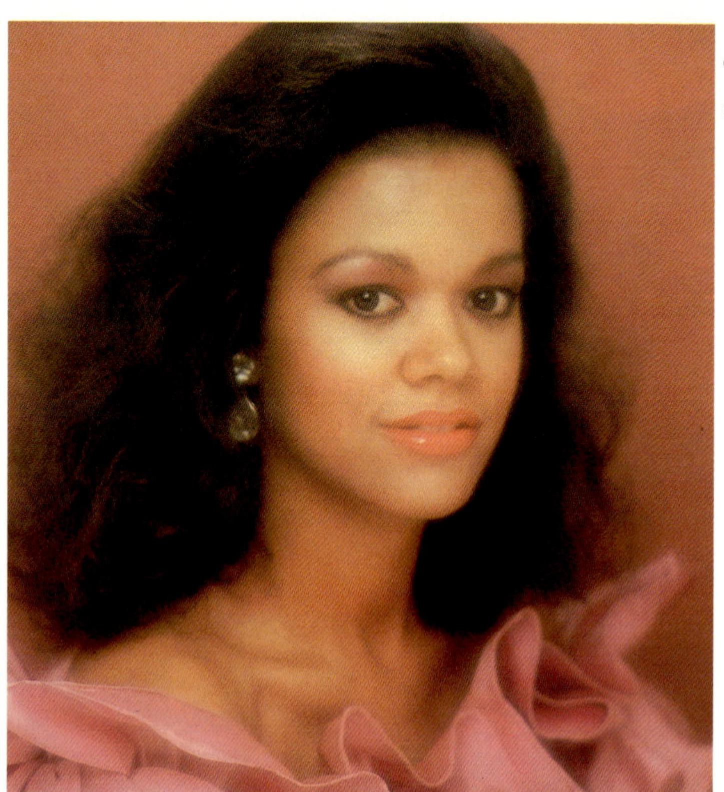
Nancy Brown

The photographer used a diffusion filter to enhance this formal portrait.

Diffusion filters. Diffusion filters work by diffusing the light to create a soft image. They are especially flattering for people with obvious skin flaws, such as wrinkles or scars, but they also flatter all by making skin glow radiantly.

You can buy three general types of diffusion filters: No. 1, 2, and 3. The weakest is the No. 1 filter, which is used primarily for portraits. The No. 2 and 3 filters, also called *mist* and *fog* filters, are most often used to create a romantic mood in scenic photographs. It is possible to purchase diffusion filters that have clear centers; these produce portraits that resemble old-fashioned cameos.

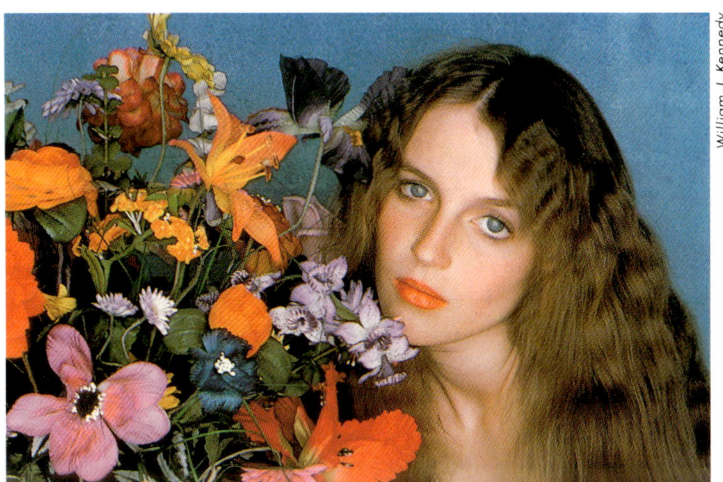

William J. Kennedy

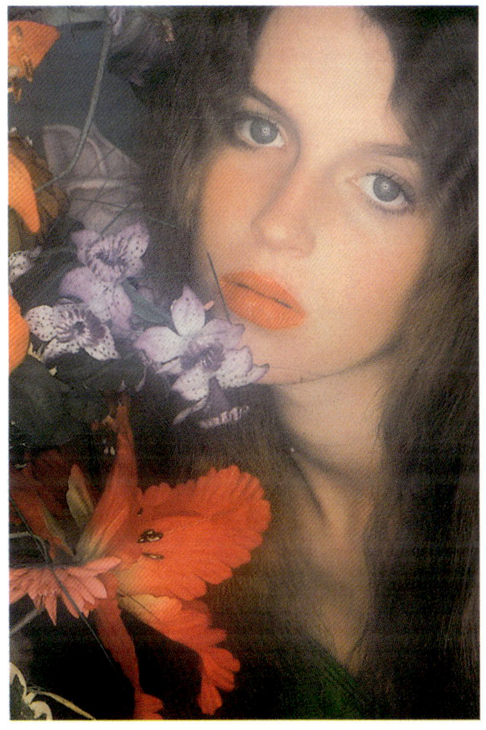

William J. Kennedy

These photographs show what a difference a diffusion filter can make. In the photograph without diffusion above, the edges of the subject and the bouquet are sharply rendered; in the diffused image, the edges are softened to create a romantic mood.

Polarizing filters. When you are photographing a scene that includes a lot of blue sky—or one in which light is reflected off the surface of water—a polarizing filter is one of the most useful accessories you can own.

A polarizing filter (also called a polarizer) works in the same way as polarizing sunglasses. It blocks light rays vibrating at a certain angle to help eliminate glare and reveal intense, saturated colors, which can heighten the drama of a photo.

Most polarizing filters contain two rings: one that remains fixed on the lens, and one that rotates. By rotating the outer ring, you can increase or lessen the polarizing effect. This effect of increasing and lessening is easy to see when you look through the filter.

Using a polarizing filter is easy if you have a single-lens-reflex (SLR) camera. All you have to do is look through the lens as you adjust the outer ring for the effect you want. If you are using a rangefinder camera, getting the effect you want is a bit trickier. Look through the filter alone as you turn the ring; then attach it to your camera, making sure that the rings stay in their same position.

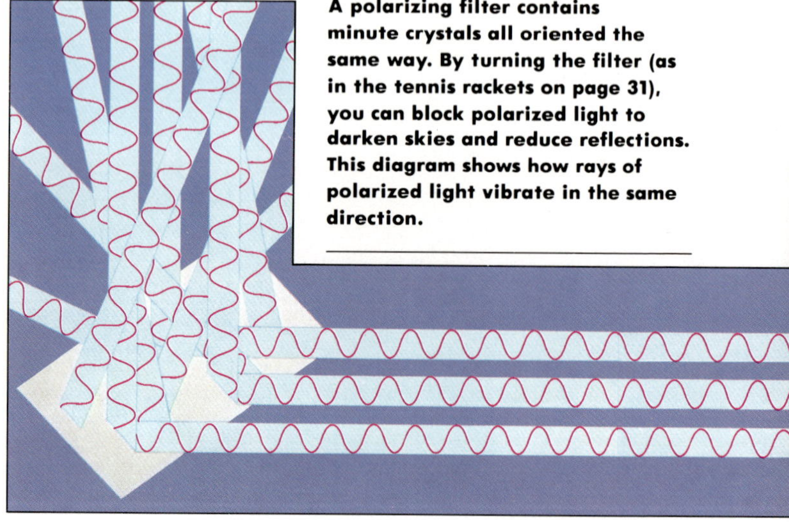

A polarizing filter contains minute crystals all oriented the same way. By turning the filter (as in the tennis rackets on page 31), you can block polarized light to darken skies and reduce reflections. This diagram shows how rays of polarized light vibrate in the same direction.

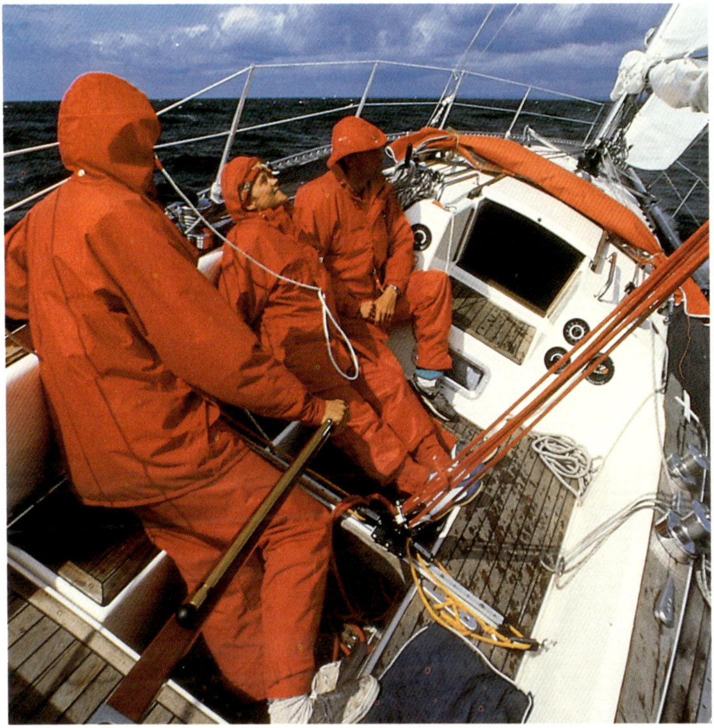

Magnus Rietz

Polarizing filters increase the color saturation, making the images more dramatic.

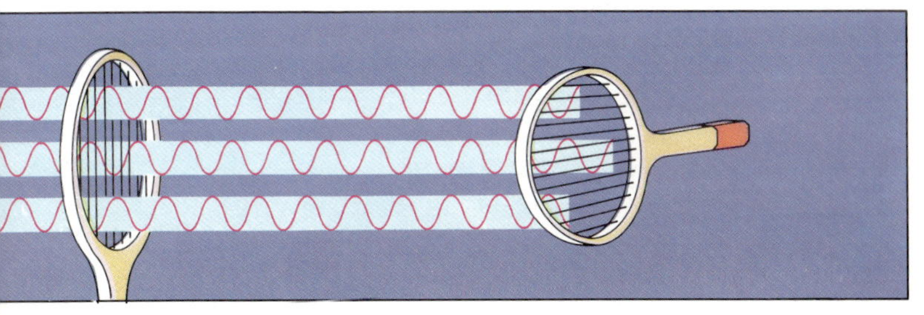

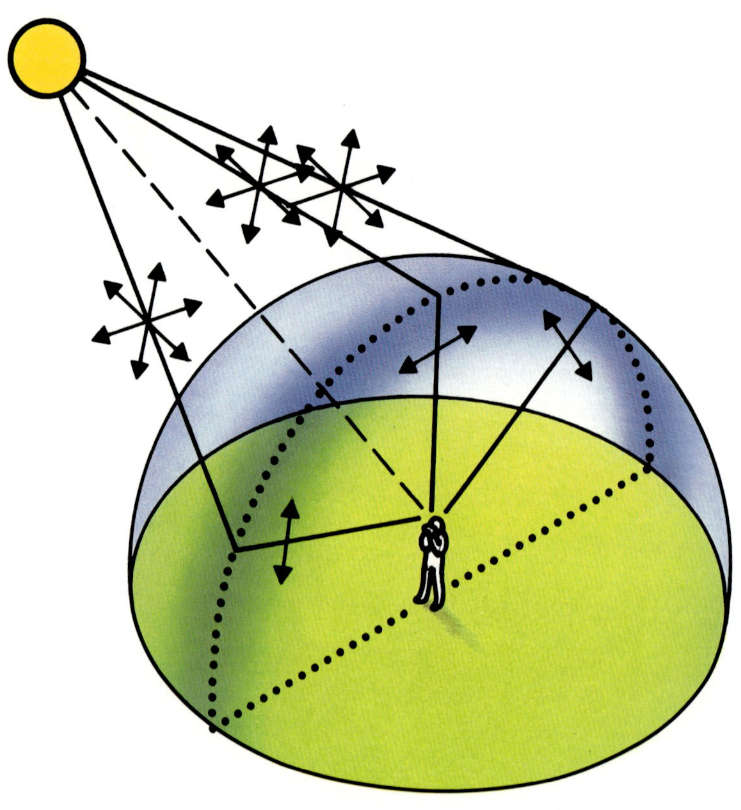

The diagram above shows the area relative to the sun in which the effect of a polarizing filter is most dramatic.

The most dramatic effect occurs when you photograph at a right angle to the sun when the sun is fairly low in the sky. Stand with your shoulder toward the sun, and look through the filter as you rotate it until you see exactly the type of effect you feel is most effective.

To reduce or eliminate reflections from a nonmetallic surface such as a window, stand at an angle of approximately 35 degrees to the reflecting surface. Rotate the polarizing filter for maximum effect at that angle.

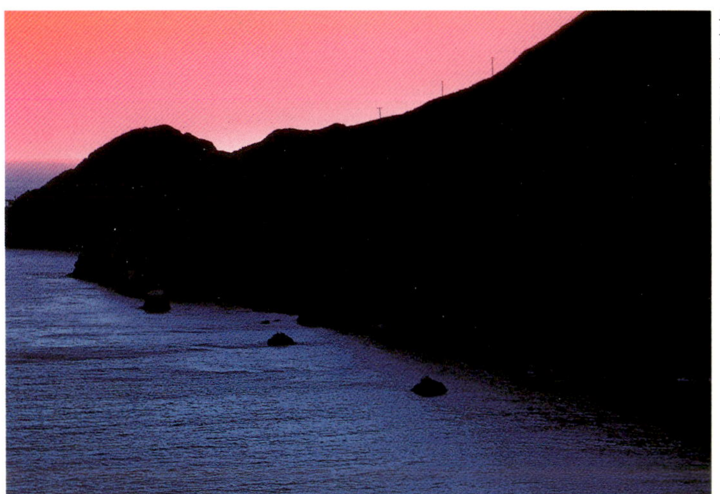

Don Landwehrle

This photograph was made with a dual-color filter. The dividing line between the colors was aligned with the natural separation of sea and sky.

Single-color and dual-color filters. Single-color filters give an overall hue to a photo, or change the colors in a scene by filtering out certain colors of light.

Color filters let you heighten the drama of your photographs. Use a red-orange filter for photos of the beach or desert to add to the impression of heat. Use a green filter to emphasize the fertility and tranquility of the forest.

Most single-color filters are available in several gradations, or densities, so you can make subtle to dramatic changes to the overall color of a scene. For example, you can use a No. 6 light-yellow filter for a slight color shift, a No. 8 yellow filter for a moderate shift, or a No. 15 deep-yellow filter for an extreme shift.

You can combine more than one filter to produce deeper color saturation or to create a different hue. However, each time you add another filter, you cut down on the amount of light that reaches the film. Therefore, you must increase your exposure to compensate for the loss by using either a larger aperture or a slower shutter speed.

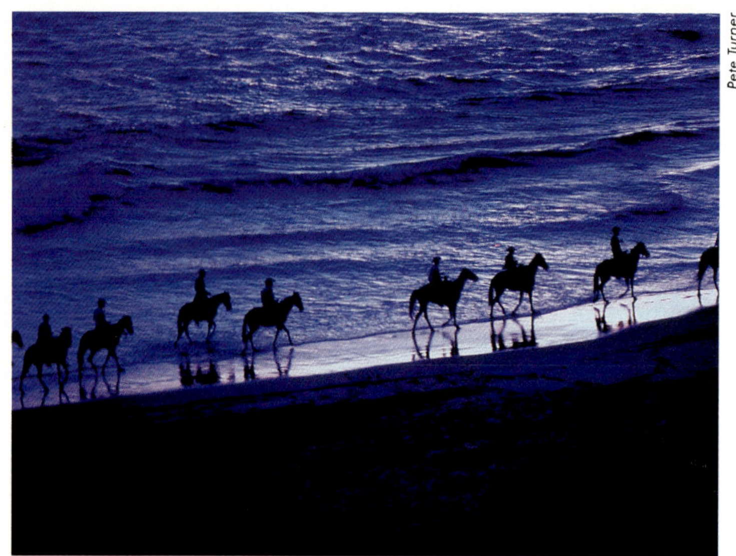

Pete Turner

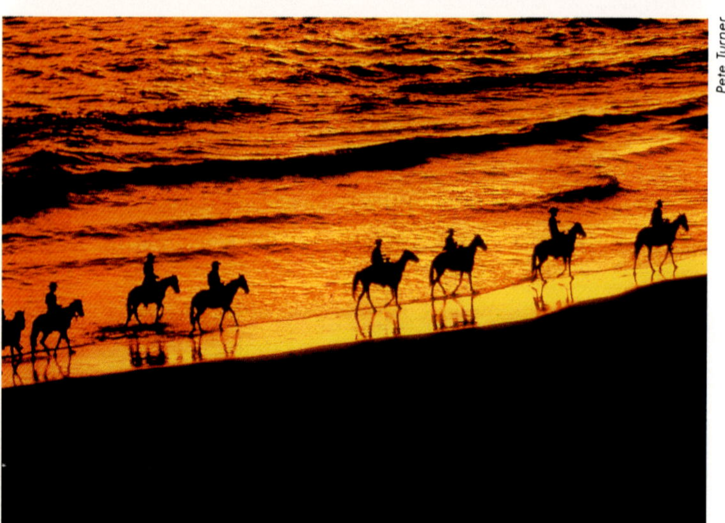

Pete Turner

Color filters can heighten the drama of a photograph. Note how the blue filter in the photograph at the top gives the scene a feeling of twilight, while the yellow filter in the lower photograph simulates a sunset.

Dual-color filters include two colors. If you hold these filters up to the light, you can easily see a line where the colors meet. To keep this line from being obvious in your photo, align it with a natural separation line or dark area in the scene. Also avoid using a small aperture with a wide-angle lens, or the dividing line may show as a fuzzy line in your photo.

Not all subjects will look attractive with all filter colors. Experiment with different colors before you shoot.

Graduated filters. Graduated filters have a colored area that gradually changes in density and a clear area. Position the clear area over the part of the scene that you want to reproduce realistically, and use the colored part to add color to the rest of the scene. For example, you could use a blue graduated filter to add color to an unattractive gray sky.

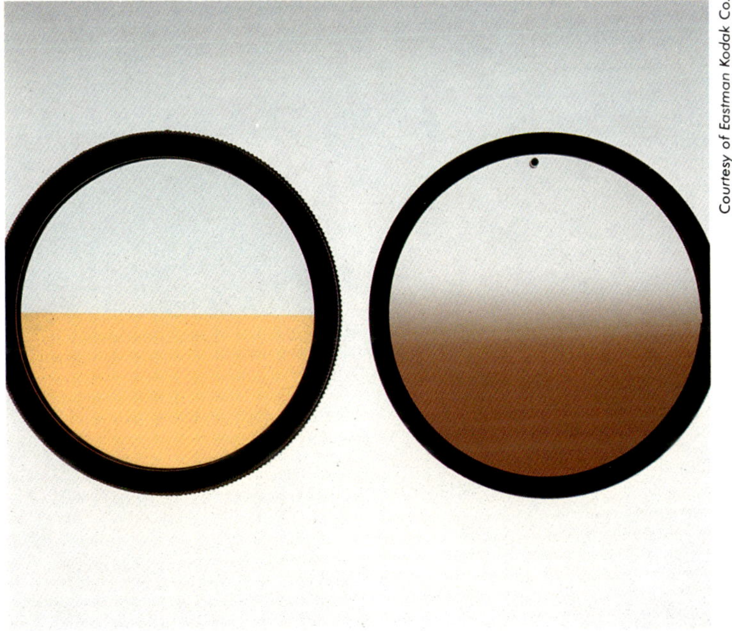

Courtesy of Eastman Kodak Co.

Dual-color filter. Graduated filter.

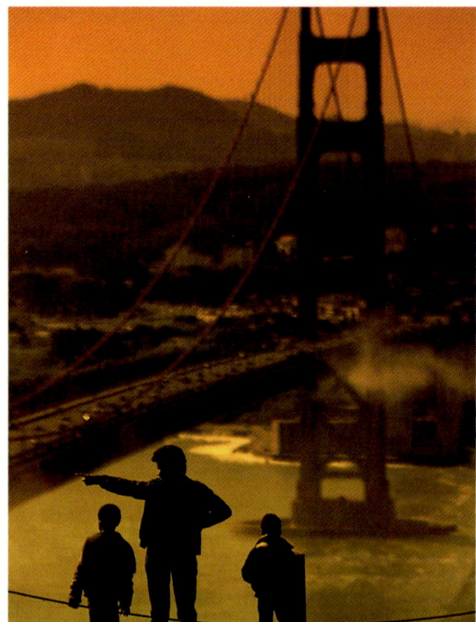

Andy Caulfield

Dual-color and graduated filters have a line that separates one color from another or from the clear part of the filter. Be sure to place the line where it will not spoil the composition of the image. Placement of the indistinct clear-color border of a graduated filter, however, is not as critical.

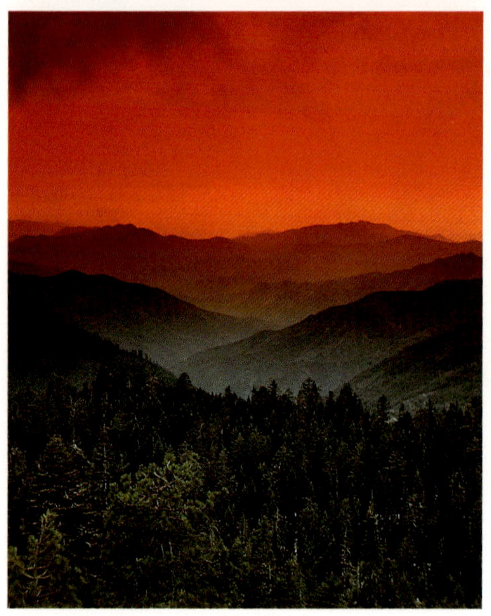

Jeff Hunter

With graduated filters, as with dual-color filters, you can vary the position of the colored areas by rotating the filters and experimenting until you get the effect you want. Although the line where the color meets the clear part of the filter is less obvious than in a dual-color filter, you should still follow the advice given for dual-color filters.

Star filters. Star filters turn point sources of light and specular highlights into stars. The stars are created by cross-hatched lines engraved on the surface of the filter. Depending on how it is constructed, a star filter will create 2- to 16-pointed stars.

The size of the star (or stars) depends on three things: the brightness of the light source in the scene, the distance from the source to your camera, and your aperture setting. Stars will be bigger when the light source is brighter and closer, and when you use a larger aperture.

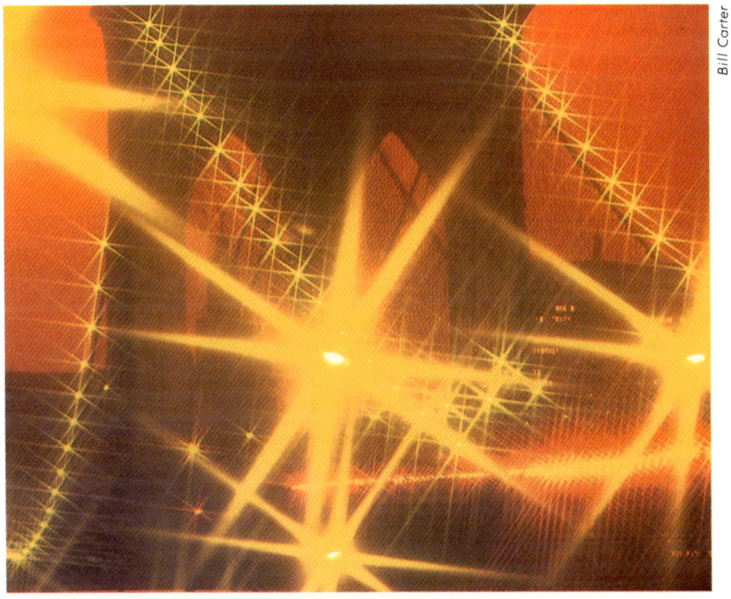

Bill Carter

You can use star filters with other filters to produce spectacular effects.

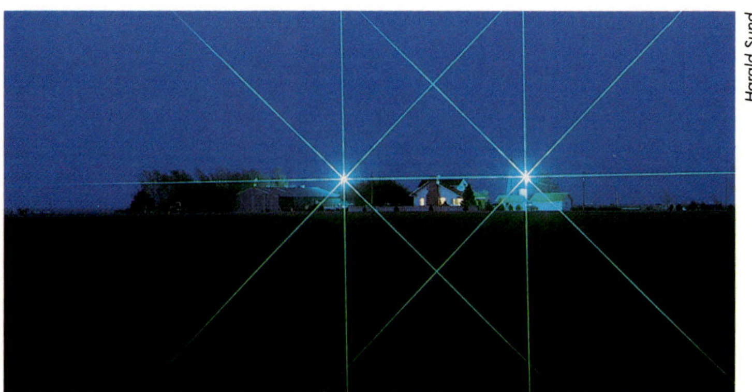

Harald Sund

Use star filters sparingly; overuse may make your pictures look gimmicky. In this photograph, the star filter makes a great contribution because it is well integrated into the overall composition.

Diffraction filters. A diffraction filter creates a rainbow-like burst around point light sources in a scene. The brighter the light source, the more pronounced the effect, particularly when the light source is against a dark background.

When you start experimenting with a diffraction filter, select as dark a background as possible, or underexpose your photographs by one or two stops (see *bracketing*, page 55) to produce the most extreme effects. Then experiment with more subtle effects by lightening the background.

Multiple-image filters. Although it is also possible to produce multiple images by making multiple exposures on the same frame of film, it is far easier to attach a multiple-image filter to your camera lens.

Multiple-image filters come in a wide variety of types; many look like cut gemstones. Some produce images in a circular, radial, or linear pattern. The linear pattern can lend an impression of motion to a still subject.

Look through your lens with the filter attached to see the effect it will produce in your photograph. Plan your images carefully to keep your picture from looking gimmicky.

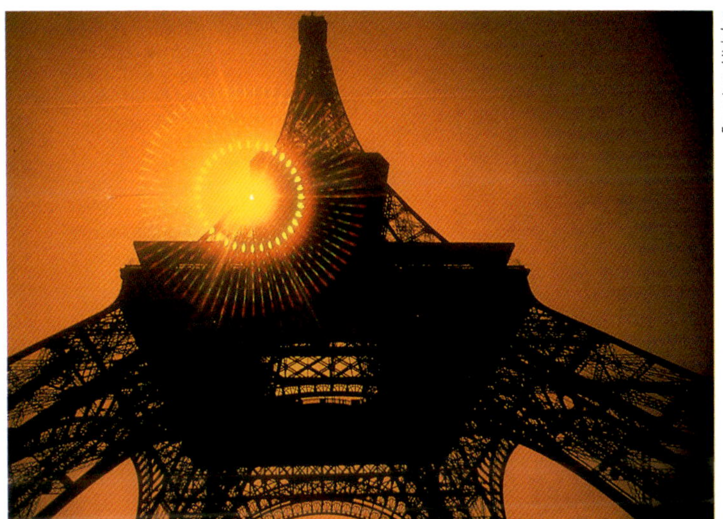

Francisco Hidalgo

In the photograph above, a diffraction filter split the light of the sun into a rainbow of colors, while in the photograph at the right, a diffraction filter was used with a multiple-image filter to produce a festive portrait of the Eiffel Tower at Christmastime.

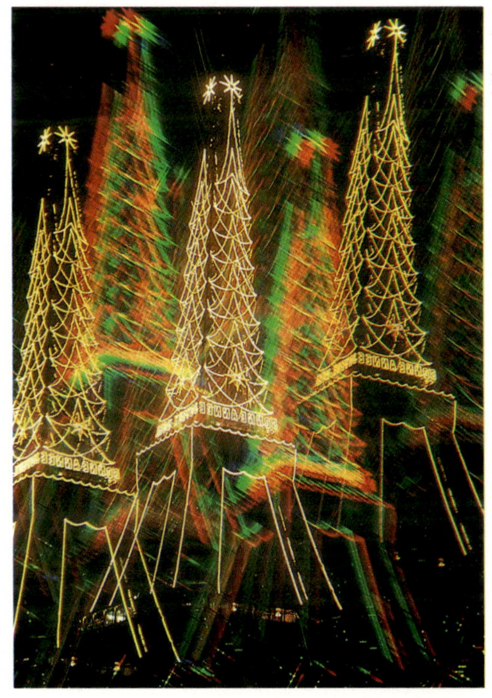

Gerard Champlong

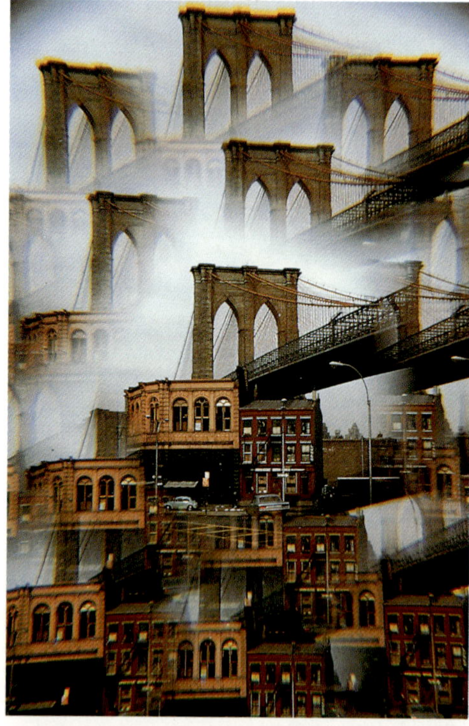

Francisco Hidalgo

The number of images you get depends on the design of your multiple-image filter. Some filters have a three-facet surface: others may have six facets.

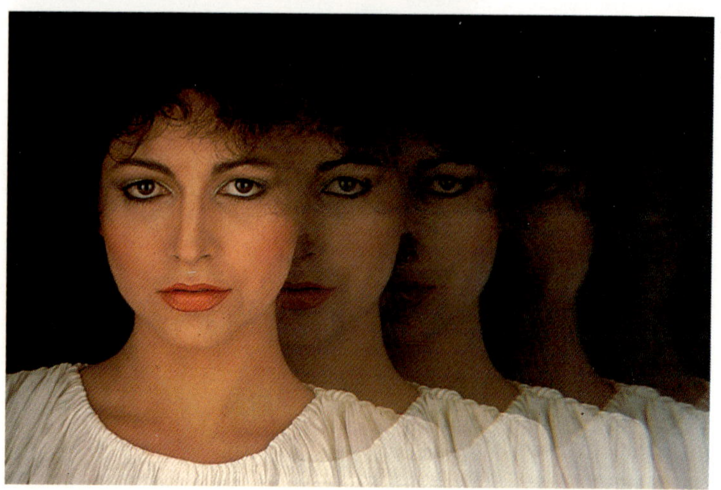

Ian Miles

Making your own filters. Any object you can see through is a potential filter. For example, glass with a carved or stippled surface may bend light or the image of your subject in an exciting and original manner. Try adding blobs of color to a piece of clear plastic with a felt-tip pen and then attaching it to a clear or UV filter to add texture and diffuse light in an interesting way.

It's easy to make a diffusion filter. Just apply streaks of petroleum jelly to a clear or UV filter in a straight or circular pattern. You can also spray hair spray onto a UV filter to create a tranquil, impressionistic effect.

Although reproducing the precisely gradated color in a graduated filter is difficult, you can easily make your own dual-color filters by placing gels of different colors on a UV filter. The results are sure to surprise and please you. As always, the key is to experiment, and learn by doing.

A handmade filter, such as a piece of textured glass, can be used to produce fantastic results. In this photograph, the action and speed of an auto race are conveyed by the distortion of lines.

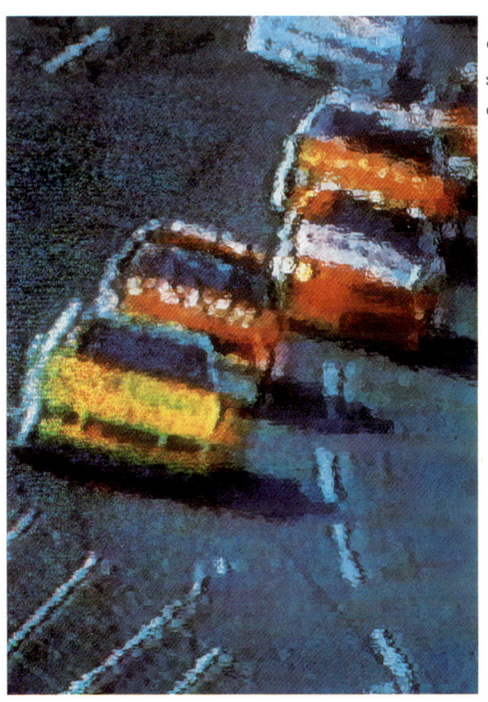

Geoffrey Gove

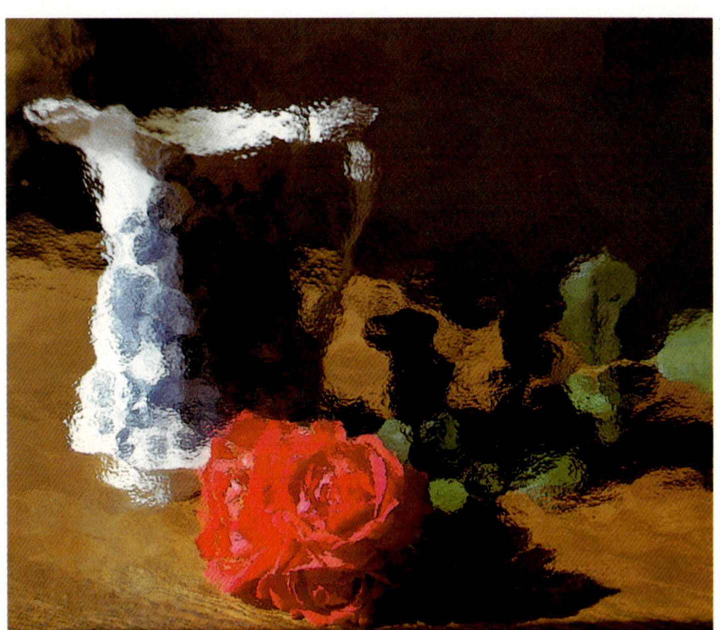
Steve Proehl

A handmade filter of textured glass can produce a "painterly" effect, as in this still-life.

You can make your own star filter by using a piece of common window screen. Hold it in front of your lens, attach it with an adapter ring, or cut it to fit inside a clear filter that screws onto your lens.

Making your own filters will give you a great deal of pride and accomplishment, and experimenting will help you understand how filters work.

SELECTIVE FOCUS

Using selective focus to show a subject in sharp focus with other elements in the scene blurred is a wonderful technique for isolating your subject against an abstract background. Use a normal or telephoto lens at a wide aperture setting to produce shallow depth of field. Selective focus renders the background as an out-of-focus tapestry of color that isolates and emphasizes the subject. It subdues objects in the background or foreground that would otherwise steal attention from your subject.

The type of lens that you use greatly affects the depth of field at any aperture setting. A normal lens (about 50 mm for a 35 mm camera) gives you great control over depth of field. At the largest aperture setting, it produces extremely shallow depth of field, and at small settings (*f*/16 or *f*/22) it gives you great depth of field.

Most people buy telephoto lenses because they make distant subjects appear larger in the film frame. However, these lenses

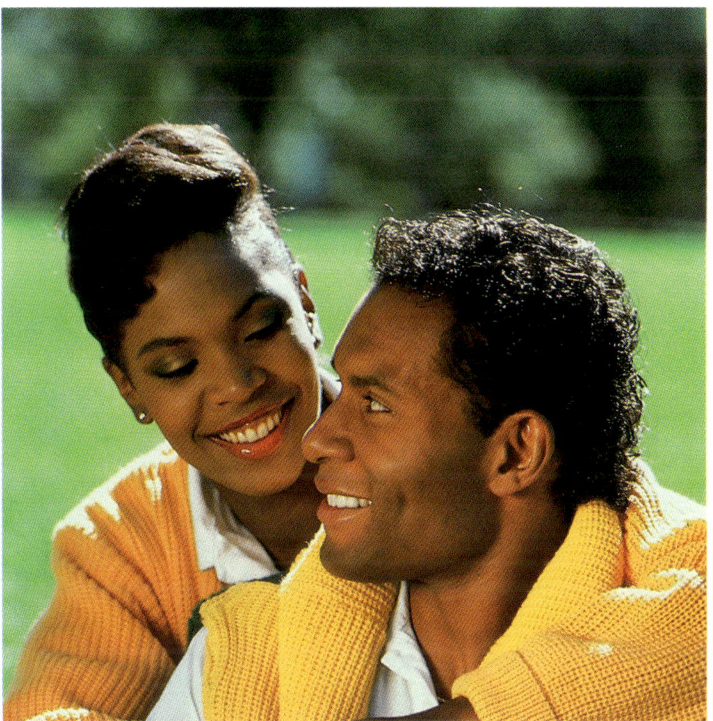

Butch Martin

By using selective focus, you can isolate your subject to produce charming portraits. Selective focus subdues background "clutter" and creates a colorful abstract background.

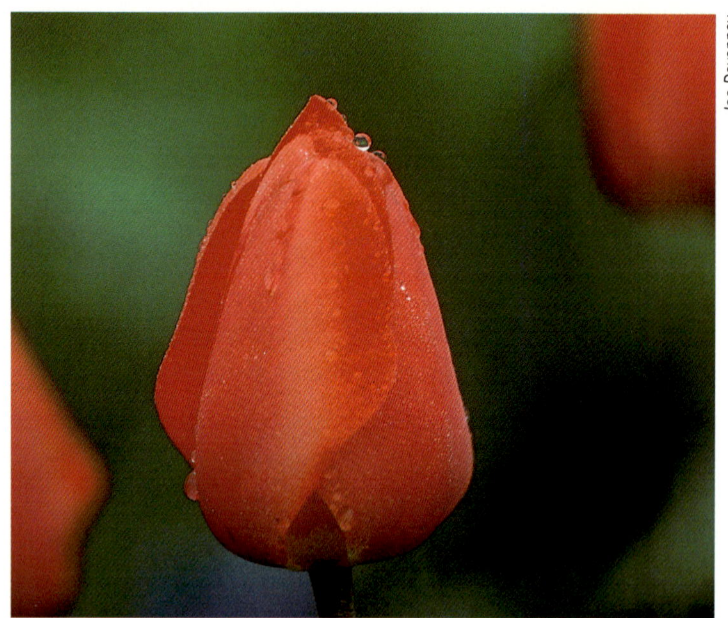

Joe Devenney

Selective focus is a popular technique for portraying flowers.

are also great for selective-focus techniques. At wide-open aperture settings, telephoto lenses produce extremely shallow depth of field; all elements in the scene that are not in the plane of focus will be blurred. The degree of blur depends on the maximum aperture of the lens, the focal length of the lens, and the camera-to-subject distance. Faster lenses, with wide maximum apertures such as *f*/2.8 or *f*/3.5, have the greatest potential for selective focus. The longer the focal length, the greater the blurred-background effect. And the closer the subject is to the camera, the shallower the depth of field.

Wide-angle lenses produce greater depth of field than other types of lenses used at the same aperture setting and subject distance, so using a wide-angle lens for selective focus can be very difficult or impossible.

When you use selective focus for portraits, always focus on your subject's eyes, the most important feature.

INTENTIONAL BLUR

For most picture-taking, you must follow the basic rule to hold the camera rock-steady—perhaps by using a tripod or bracing it in some other way—to get the sharpest, clearest images. But when you're ready to try new, creative techniques of intentionally blurring your image, it's time to break this rule!

In this section, we discuss the techniques of *panning* your camera, which creates a blur in the background of your photograph (and sometimes the foreground as well); and *zooming* the lens during exposure, which creates the effect shown in the photographs on pages 48 and 49. The aim of both techniques is to create a feeling of motion in the image.

Panning the camera. Did you ever try to snap a picture of a marathon runner only to produce a blur against a perfectly sharp background? Or maybe you used flash or a very fast shutter speed to freeze a moving subject, and were disappointed that it looked static, without a sense of motion.

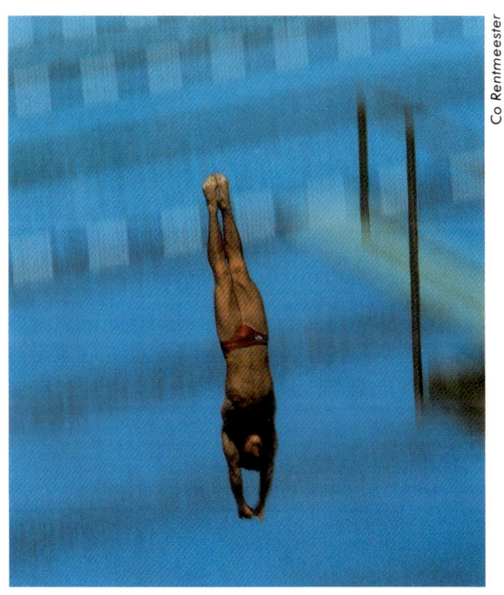

Co Rentmeester

Panning, like selective focus, can isolate your subject against an indistinct, abstract background.

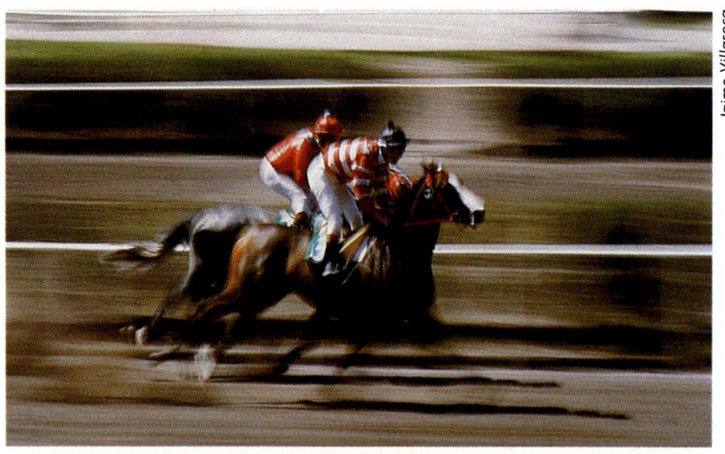

Jaime Villaseca

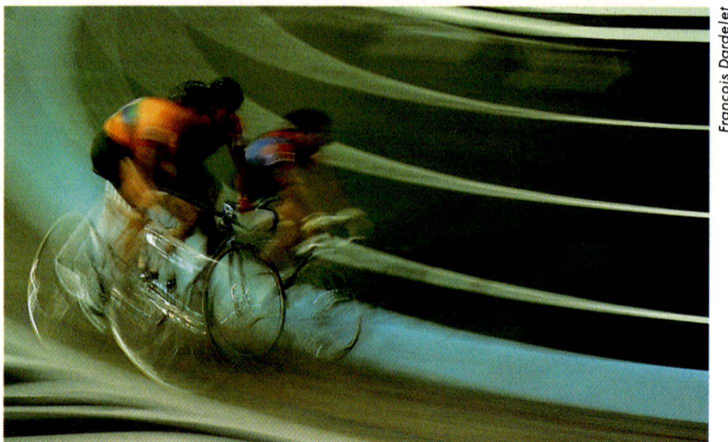

François Dardelet

Panning is an ideal technique to use with such action subjects as racehorses and bicyclists.

You can make an effective photo of this kind of moving subject. To capture both a clear image of a racer and a feeling of motion, try moving the camera to follow the racer as you take your picture. This technique, called panning, can create excellent representations of motion in a still image. By panning, you can show a runner or a car frozen against a streaked back-

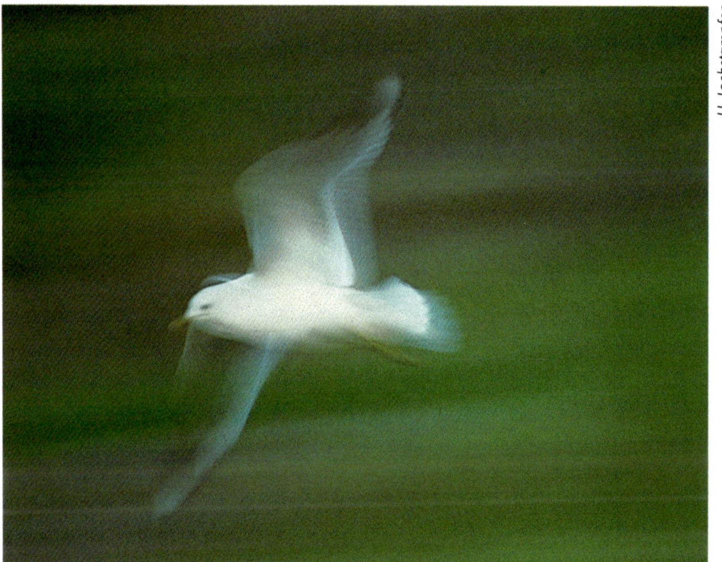

U. Lochstampfer

Panning with nature subjects in action can produce impressionistic renderings, as in this photograph of a bird in flight.

ground; or you can move your camera to create the impression of motion in stationary objects—for example, by portraying bright lights as streaks across a dark night sky.

To pan your camera, move it smoothly to keep your moving subject in one position in the viewfinder while the shutter is open. You can achieve effects ranging from an abstract blur across the entire frame to a sharp subject against a streaked, blurred background. The effect in your picture depends on three things:

SUCCESSFUL PANNING DEPENDS ON . . .

- how fast your subject is moving
- the distance from the camera to the subject
- the shutter speed

When you use longer shutter speeds, such as 1/60 or 1/125 second, the results can be difficult to predict, because you increase your chances of jiggling the camera in addition to panning. But these shutter speeds also allow you to produce great photos that record some movement in your subject even as you pan to keep it positioned in the viewfinder. For example, you can record a mostly sharp image of a racehorse with blurred hooves that convey a feeling of great speed. Experiment with different shutter speeds until you feel confident with this technique.

Zooming the lens during exposure. Most people buy a zoom lens in place of two or more fixed-focal-length lenses, and set the lens at a single focal length to make each exposure. But a zoom lens can do more than save you the cost of extra lenses! You can change the focal-length setting of the lens during the exposure if you use an exposure time that is long enough. The effects of this technique can change an ordinary scene into a dynamic image.

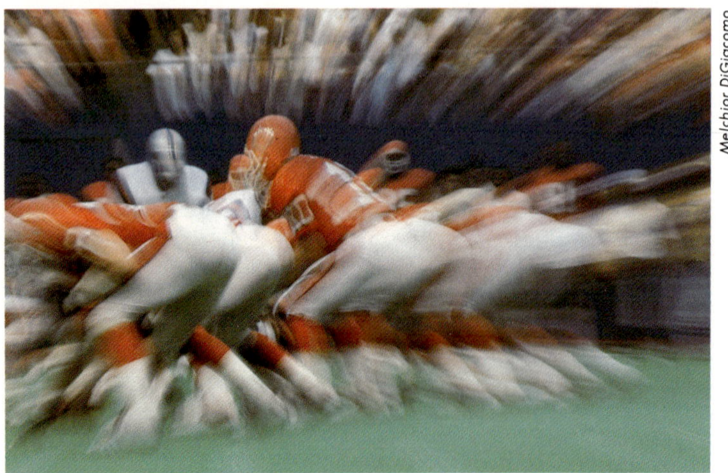

Melchior DiGiacomo

Zooming during exposure helps to isolate the center of action, as in this football play.

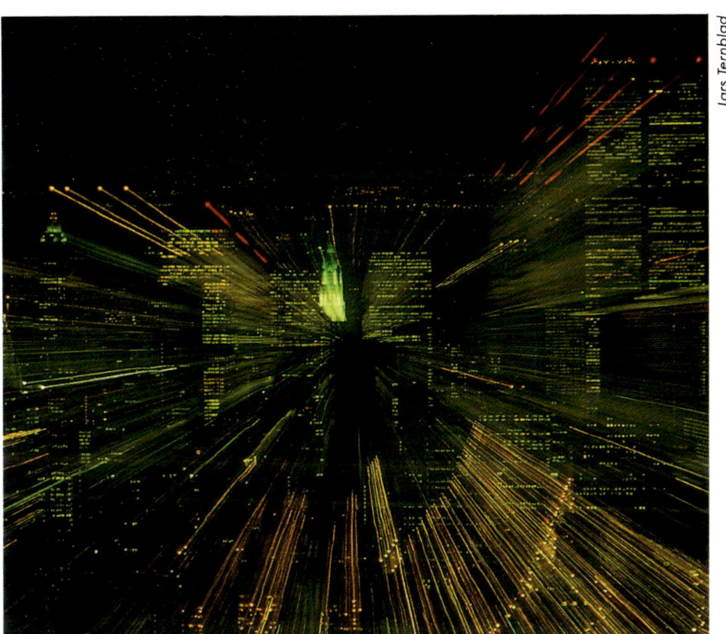
Lars Ternblad

Zooming creates an impression of radiating energy.

While panning will give you streaks moving in one direction, zooming during exposure creates strong lines radiating out from the center of interest, which can give a striking sense of motion. The degree of the effect depends on the focal-length range of the zoom lens, how much of that range you cover during the exposure, and the shutter speed. You must use a slow shutter speed—1/30 second or slower—so place your camera on a tripod.

Before you make the exposure, examine the scene at the longest and shortest focal-length settings of the lens to be sure that you're not including unwanted objects in the frame. You'll need to expose the main subject or center of interest long enough before zooming the lens to make it clearly identifiable. Keep the lens at the shortest focal length for half the exposure time, and then zoom to the longest focal length.

UNUSUAL EXPOSURES

The exposure that your film receives when you take a photograph depends on *aperture* and *shutter speed*. Your aperture setting determines the intensity of the light that reaches the film, and your shutter speed determines how long light is allowed to strike the film. Most single-lens-reflex (SLR) cameras will allow you to experiment creatively with both aperture and shutter speed to make startling and exciting images.

In this section, we will discuss such techniques as multiple exposures, existing-light exposures at night, and intentional overexposure.

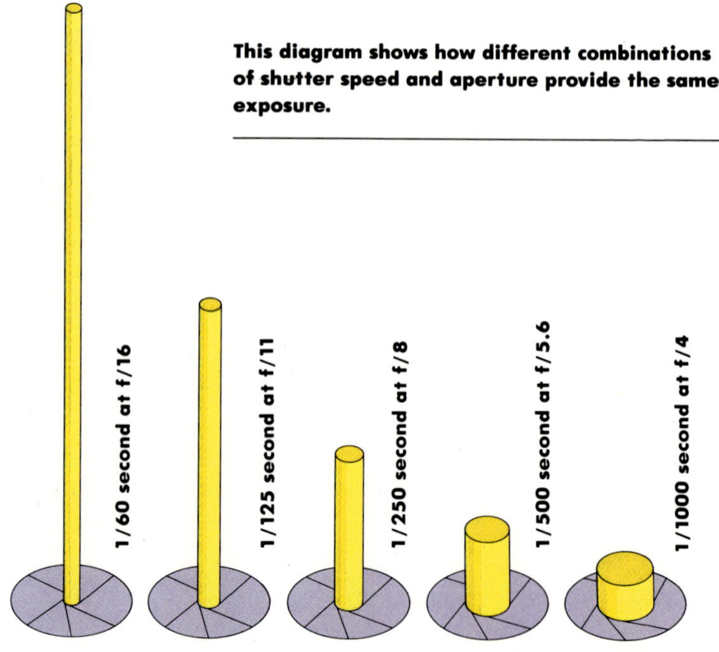

This diagram shows how different combinations of shutter speed and aperture provide the same exposure.

Multiple exposures. If your camera has a multiple-exposure button that lets you make successive exposures on the same frame of film, you can easily create *multiple exposures*. Simply engage the multiple-exposure button according to the instructions in your camera manual. If your camera has a manual film-advance lever, you can make multiple exposures even if the camera doesn't have a multiple-exposure button. After you make the first exposure, engage the film-rewind button as you move the film-advance lever to cock the shutter. You can then make your second exposure on the same frame.

You can make multiple exposures over the entire film frame, as in the photograph of the tennis player at the right, or over part of the frame, as shown below.

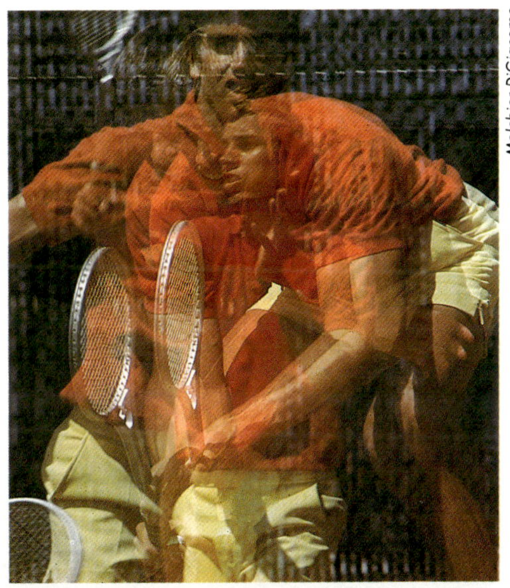

Melchior DiGiacomo

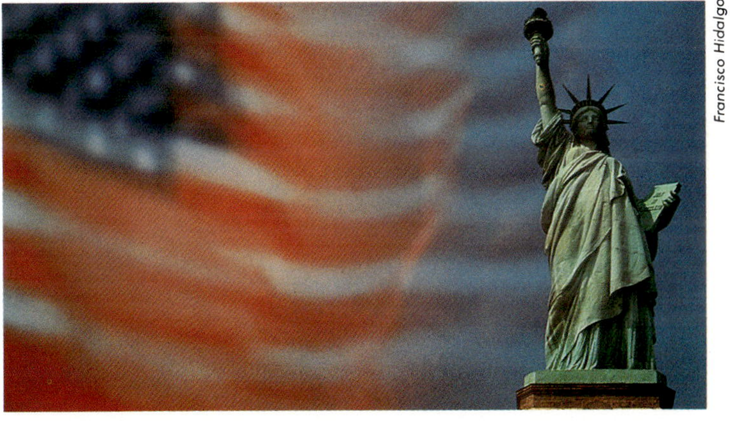

Francisco Hidalgo

Some multiple exposures cover the entire film frame and some are placed in selected areas within the frame, but they work in much the same way. Light tones of an image will appear only in darker areas of a previously exposed scene. Light areas superimposed on other light areas will wash out; dark areas on top of dark areas will contain little image detail.

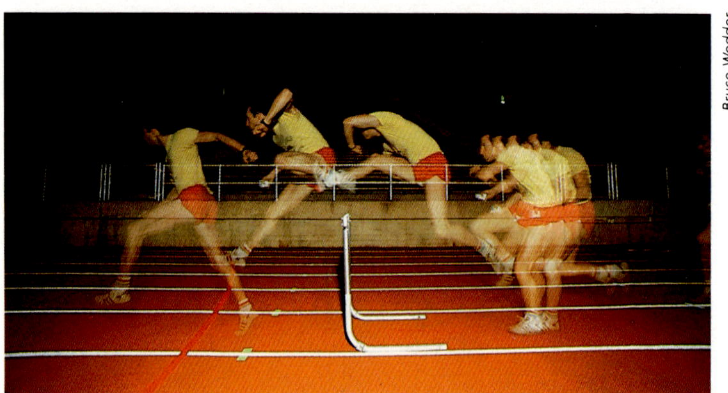

Bruce Wodder

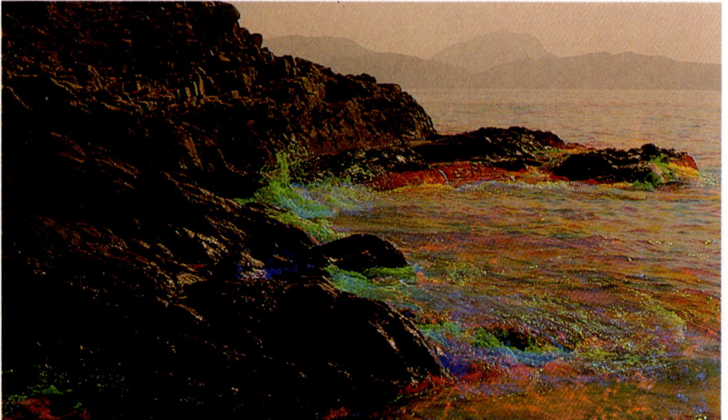

Yan Lun Jean Yves

Multiple exposures can isolate many distinct actions of a subject in motion, as shown in the photo of a hurdlers' jump at the top. Above, each separate exposure was made with a different color filter to record color in the moving water. The shore looks normal because the effects of the filters combined to "recreate" white light.

If you use the entire frame to create a multiple exposure—that is, if you superimpose one image on top of another across the entire picture area—you must adjust each exposure to prevent the film from being overexposed. When you make two exposures, you must cut the normally calculated setting for each exposure in half, by reducing it by one stop. To do this, use the next higher shutter speed or the next smaller aperture. If you have an automatic camera, you can adjust the film-speed setting (the ISO number) to twice the speed of your film. If you superimpose four exposures on the same frame, you must reduce the exposure for each image by a factor of two—that is, use an aperture two stops smaller, a shutter speed four times as high, or an ISO setting four times the normal speed.

Another way to make multiple exposures is to insert specific lighter-toned objects or areas into dark areas of the original scene. For example, suppose that you are shooting a portrait of someone wearing black clothes sitting against a black background. Your first exposure can be a classic three-quarter portrait. Then for the second exposure, you can place a light image in the dark area of the original image. You may choose something that helps reveal your subject's character, such as a kitten or a favorite keepsake. Or you might expose his or her face again in a dark area of the frame.

If you remember to expose light areas onto dark areas, no exposure compensation will be necessary. Adding an isolated bright object to a darker area generally does not cause overexposure in the darker area.

Multiple exposures of a moving subject made at regular intervals on the same frame can create a dramatic effect. You can do this best by shooting with an electronic flash against a dark or black background. Keep the shutter open on the B (bulb) setting as you fire the flash repeatedly at the moving subject.

One of the best ways to make stunning fireworks photographs is to let the individual bursts make their own multiple exposures on the film. Mount your camera on a tripod so that the field of view of the lens covers the area where the fireworks will be.

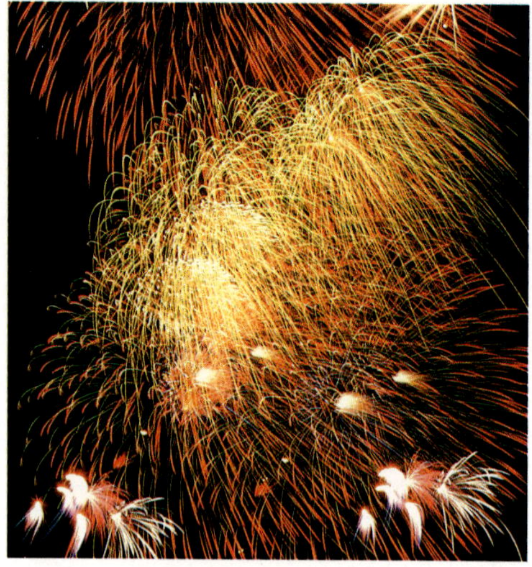

Jake Rajs

By making multiple exposures, you can fill the frame with many individual images of fireworks.

One of the best ways to make stunning fireworks photographs is to let the individual bursts make their own multiple exposures on the film. Mount your camera on a tripod so that the field of view of the lens covers the area where the fireworks will be. Set the aperture for the speed of the film you are using (see the chart on page 57 for starting points) and keep the shutter open for several seconds to several minutes to capture as many individual bursts as you like. If the picture area includes other sources of light, you'll have to limit the exposure time to avoid overexposure.

Night exposures. Subjects for night or twilight exposures can vary greatly, from silhouettes against a sunset to city lights or patterns formed by traffic on a highway. Night exposures range from a fraction of a second to many minutes, depending on the type of scene, the speed of your lens, film speed, and so on. However, at exposure times of one second or longer, you may notice a change in the response of the film to light. At these long exposure times, the effective speed of your film decreases, and color films may show color-balance changes. You must make an exposure adjustment to compensate for the loss of film speed.

The chart on page 57 provides exposure adjustments for several different film types and exposure times.

Using filters such as KODAK Color Compensating (CC) Filters can help correct color shifts that can occur at long exposure times. However, when color rendition isn't critical, it's usually impractical to use filters, which absorb light and may require even longer exposure times.

When you're uncertain about your exposure settings, *bracket* your exposures. Bracketing simply means taking extra pictures of the scene at different exposure settings. For nighttime exposures, bracket by at least two stops over and under the exposure indicated by your meter or the recommended exposure. Although this may use a little more film and time, it will help you get pleasing results under almost any conditions. "Correct" exposure for night photographs is largely a matter of personal preference.

For most night photography, a steady camera is essential. At the slow shutter speeds you'll often be using, mount the camera on a sturdy tripod, or brace it on any stable surface—a wall, a bench, a mailbox, or a car. A cable release will let you trip the shutter without jarring the camera. Or you can use the self-timer to release the shutter. If you have a single-lens-reflex (SLR) camera that allows you to lock up the mirror, do so after com-

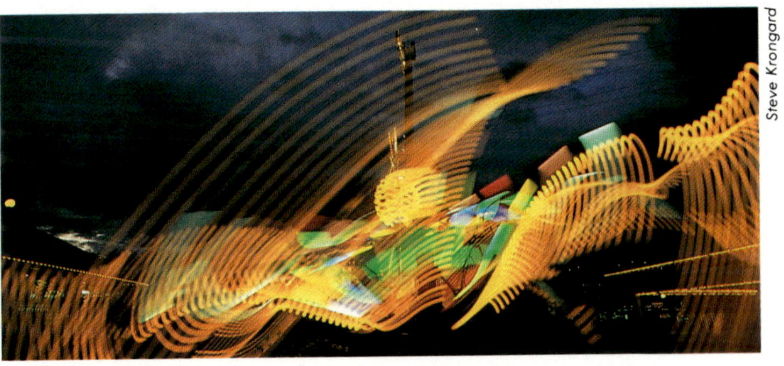
Steve Krongard

This intentional blur of a carnival ride shows how effectively a colorful, festive scene can be portrayed by time exposure.

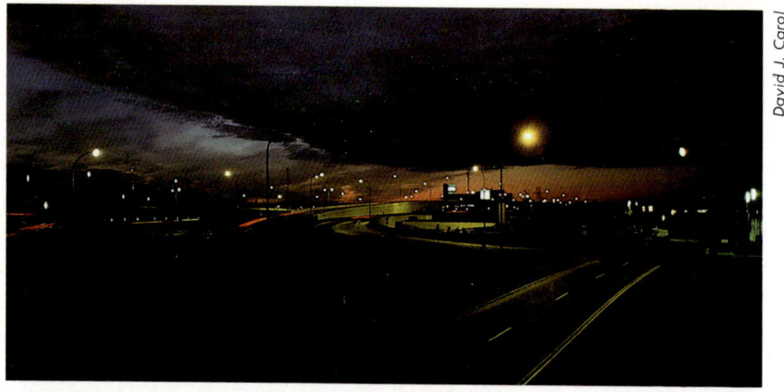

David J. Carol

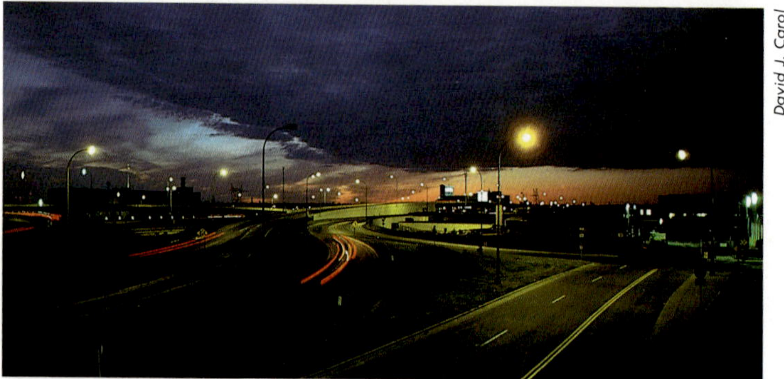

David J. Carol

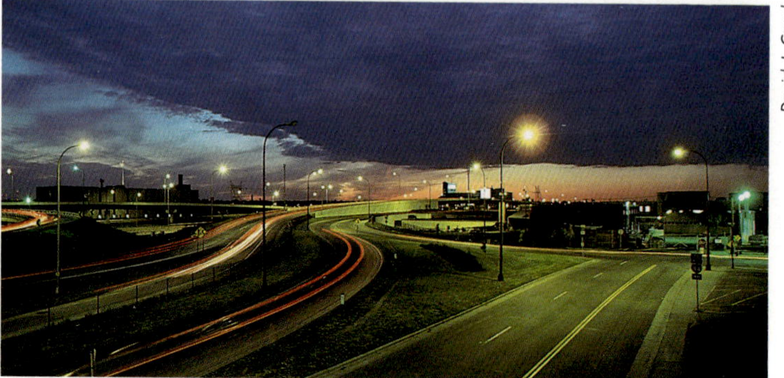

David J. Carol

Traffic is a favorite subject for night exposures; cars turn into streaming ribbons of light. The top photograph was exposed for 1 second, the middle for 4 seconds, and the bottom for 15 seconds.

SUGGESTED EXPOSURES FOR SOME NIGHTTIME SCENES*					
Picture Subjects	**KODACHROME 64 EKTACHROME 100 HC KODACOLOR GOLD 100 EKTAR 125**	**EKTACHROME 200 EKTACHROME 160 KODACHROME 200 KODACOLOR GOLD 200**	**EKTACHROME 400 EKTACHROME 200 EKTACHROME 160 † KODACOLOR GOLD 400**	**EKTAR 1000 EKTACHROME P800/1600 Professional at EI 800‡ EKTACHROME 400†**	**KODACOLOR GOLD 1600**
Brightly lighted downtown street scenes (Wet streets make interesting reflections.)	1/30 sec *f*/2	1/30 sec *f*/2.8	1/60 sec *f*/2.8	1/60 sec *f*/4	1/125 sec *f*/4
Brightly lighted nightclub or theatre districts—Las Vegas or Times Square	1/30 sec *f*/2.8	1/30 sec *f*/4	1/60 sec *f*/4	1/125 sec *f*/4	1/250 sec *f*/4
Floodlighted buildings, fountains, monuments	1 sec *f*/4	1/2 sec *f*/4	1/15 sec *f*/2	1/30 sec *f*/2	1/30 sec *f*/2.8
Fairs, amusement parks at night	1/15 sec *f*/2	1/30 sec *f*/2	1/30 sec *f*/2.8	1/60 sec *f*/2.8	1/60 sec *f*/4
Skyline—10 minutes after sunset	1/30 sec *f*/4	1/60 sec *f*/4	1/60 sec *f*/5.6	1/125 sec *f*/5.6	1/125 sec *f*/8
Aerial fireworks displays—Keep camera shutter open on BULB for several bursts.	*f*/8	*f*/11	*f*/16	*f*/22	*f*/22

*For color balance of film, see the chart on page 66.

†You can increase the speed of KODAK EKTACHROME 400, 200, and 160 Films in 135 size 2 times by having them push-processed when you return the film for processing.

‡KODAK EKTACHROME P800/1600 Professional Film (Daylight) can be rated at EI 800 with 1-stop push-processing (Push 1), at EI 1600 with 2-stop push-processing arranged by your photo dealer, and sometimes even at EI 3200. To use the EI 1600 film speed, merely *decrease* suggested exposure in this column by one stop, at EI 3200 *decrease* exposure by *two* stops.

posing your photo and setting the exposure. Then allow the camera to settle for a few seconds on the tripod before you release the shutter.

Intentional overexposure and underexposure. As you may have noticed from your bracketed night shots, variations in exposure can make a great difference in the appearance of a scene. Slightly overexposing your film lightens dark tones and produces a more open, airy, and pastel effect. In landscapes, for example, overexposure can accentuate atmospheric effects such as fog and haze, and increase the feeling of distance. In portraits, slight overexposure can lighten facial tones and reduce character lines to create a "flawless" subject.

The best way to explore subtle variations in exposure is to use color transparency (slide) film. Exposure is far more critical with slide films, because the processed film is the finished photo-

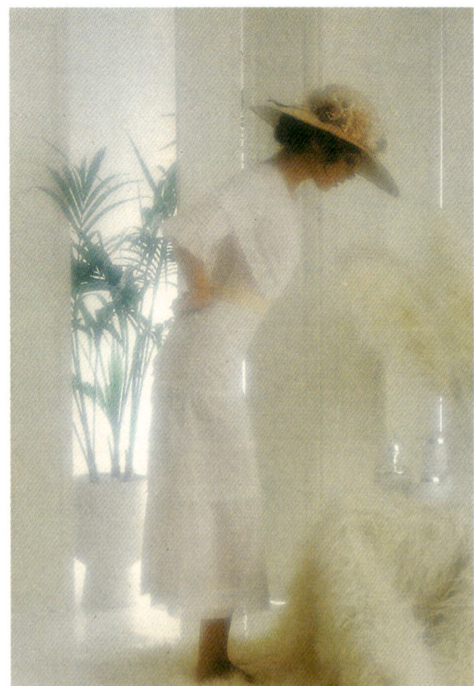
Larry Dale Gordon

Intentional overexposure, as shown by the top photograph, can render subjects flawless by reducing detail; intentional underexposure can deepen colors and shadows.

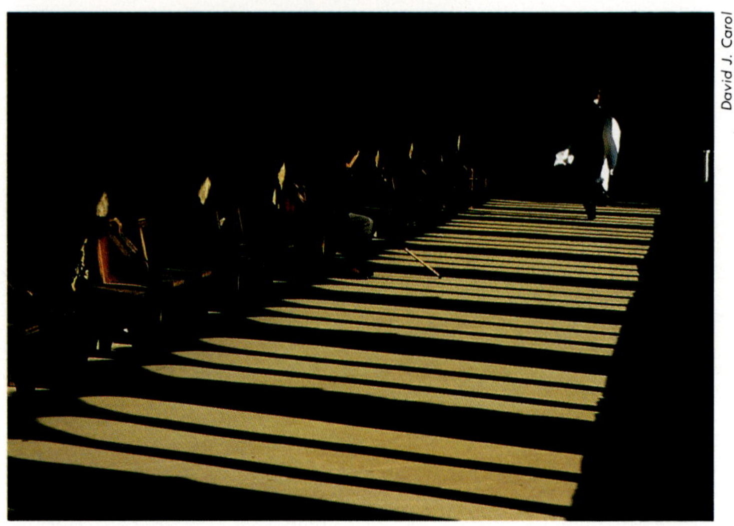
David J. Carol

graph. No exposure corrections can be made during printing, as they can with color negative films.

When you overexpose slide film, be very careful not to go too far. In general, overexposing by one stop will lighten the tones enough; at two stops over, highlights may lose all detail and shadows may have a smoky, unreal appearance. Experiment to discover the effects of overexposure.

If your camera has an exposure-compensation dial, make images with a slight degree of overexposure by setting the dial at "+1/2" or "+1." Recheck your camera manual to be sure you know how to use this control. With an automatic camera that doesn't have an exposure-compensation dial, you can readjust the ISO setting on your camera to half the film speed. For example, if you're using a film with a speed of ISO 200, set the film-speed dial at 100. If you have a manual camera, just increase your calculated exposure by one stop.

While overexposure yields lighter tones that can soften the appearance of your subject, intentional underexposure darkens the scene and can exaggerate subtle details in the highlights. Both colors and shadows deepen.

Intentional underexposure can be extremely effective in scenes that include bright colors and strong shadows. Color slides of seascapes in bright sunlight, sunrises, and sunsets frequently benefit from underexposure by one or two stops. Colors become richly saturated, and shadowed foregrounds appear as bold silhouettes. To determine your exposure for such interpretations, meter only the brightest part of the scene—the sky or water.

As with intentional overexposure, don't go too far. Although darker slides often increase dramatic impact and reveal greater detail in highlight areas, the loss of shadow detail and clean whites may produce murky, unflattering results. When in doubt as to how much you should underexpose a scene for a dramatic effect, make a series of exposures in half-stop increments from the normal exposure indicated by your meter to about two stops less than normal.

PART THREE

CREATIVE TECHNIQUES WITH FILM

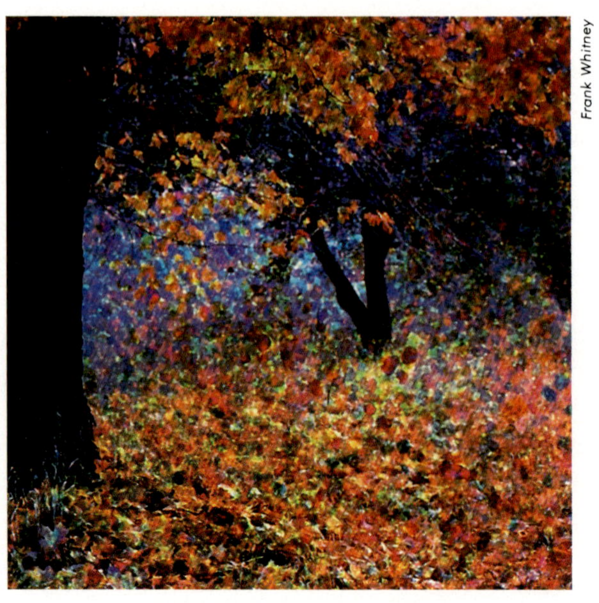

Frank Whitney

You can apply many creative techniques to film both before and after it has been processed, and cropping (see page 21) is only one of them! Just as you may have thought that there was only one right way of taking a picture, you may still have limiting ideas about film, film developing, and creating a final image.

In Part Three, we'll discuss using films creatively, as well as the techniques of "pushing" film to achieve enhanced grain and making slide "sandwiches." These techniques will expand your creative horizons.

TYPES OF FILM AND THEIR USES

When you purchase film at your local supermarket or drugstore, you will probably have to choose from color-slide films or color-negative films that are balanced for daylight.

But the wide variety of films that are available in camera stores include many more than just daylight-balanced films—more than we have room to discuss in this book. We will, however, discuss color films balanced for daylight and for tungsten light and learn how to use them for special effects. We'll also touch on black-and-white films such as KODAK T-MAX Professional Films and KODAK High Speed Infrared Film. This will give you an understanding of the wide selection of films and their uses.

Using the "wrong" film. Getting photos with an orange or blue cast back from the lab is a common problem. These color casts occur when you use a film balanced for one type of light under a different light source. Although you should always know which film is "correct" for each lighting situation, using the wrong film intentionally can produce striking effects.

Why are so many types of film available? Our eyes convince us that we are seeing the same kind of light most of the time, although we do see differing levels of it. Film, on the other hand, is made to record different *colors* of light; when a film is not matched to its proper light source, it produces color casts that are often obvious and sometimes unacceptable. The actual

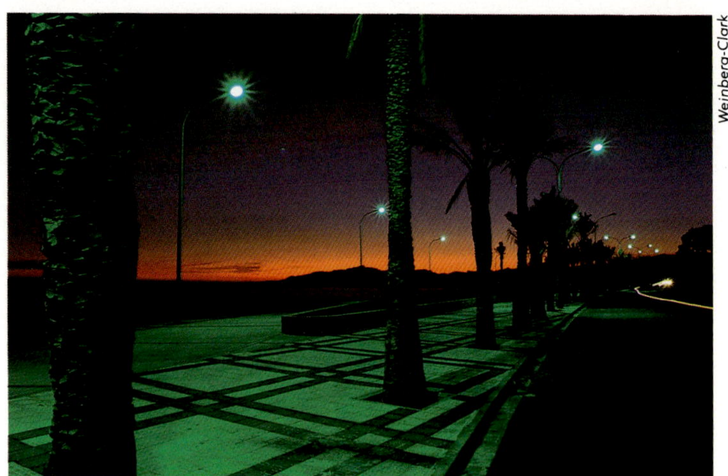

Pictures made on tungsten film outdoors in daylight normally have a blue cast. Using tungsten film under mercury-vapor lights results in an eery and provocative scenic, as shown above.

color of a light source is called its *color temperature*. The higher the color temperature, the more blue-white the light; the lower the color temperature, the more orange-red the light. The color temperature of daylight at midday is 5500 K (the K stands for degrees *Kelvin*).

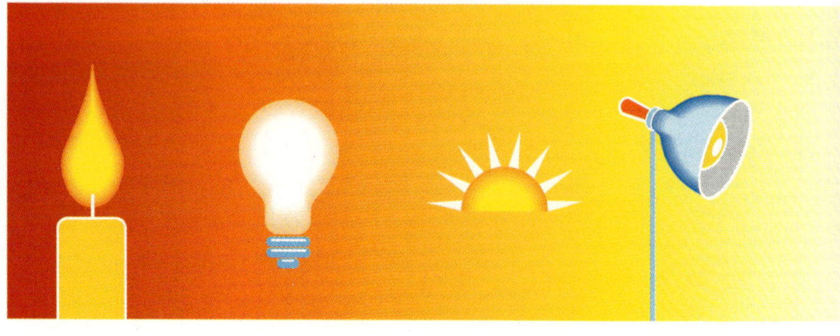

Almost all films for color prints are balanced for exposure to daylight or electronic flash, but they also give pleasing results under most existing-light conditions. Films such as KODAK EKTAR 1000 and KODACOLOR GOLD 1600 Films feature improved sensitivity to tungsten light.

Interior incandescent lighting has a substantially lower color temperature than daylight. When you photograph subjects under incandescent lighting on a daylight slide film, they will have an orange cast. Color-slide films that are specially balanced for artificial light are tungsten films (named for the filament material in normal household light bulbs) and Type A films. Tungsten films, such as KODAK EKTACHROME 160 Film (Tungsten), give excellent results under common household lamps. KODACHROME 40 Film (Type A) is designed for exposure with photolamps (3400 K).

Interior fluorescent lighting presents a different problem: your pictures are likely to turn out with a green cast. All films require special filters or combinations of filters to eliminate this cast. However, exact color balance is difficult to achieve, because it's often hard to find out what kind of fluorescent lamps are used.

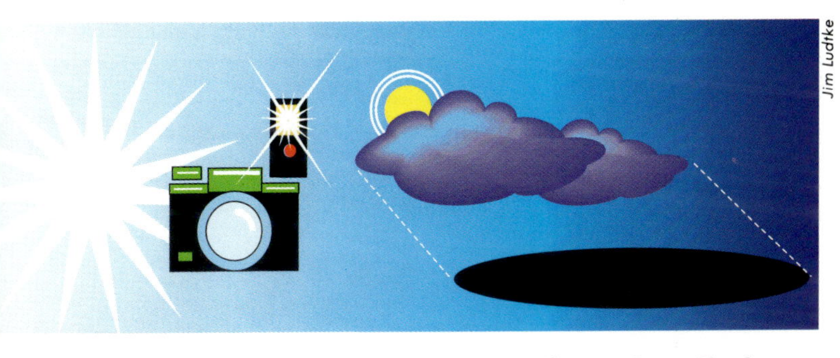
Jim Ludtke

Daylight
5500 K
Electronic Flash
5500-6000 K

Overcast Sky
7000 K

Open Shade
12000-18000 K

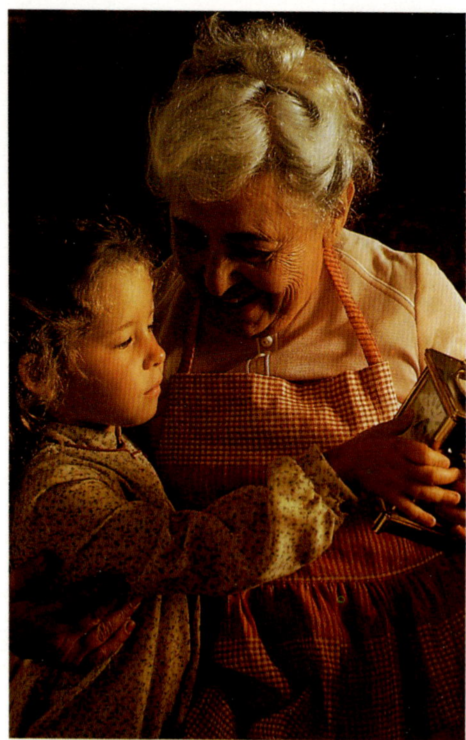

Elyse Lewin

Daylight film used indoors has a yellow to orange cast, which can flush skin tones with a warm glow.

When people mismatch their film and light source, they often don't like the results at all. But if you are aware of the effects of mismatching, you can use these color alterations to your advantage. Scenes under tungsten lighting that are photographed on daylight film may resemble outdoor scenes shot at dawn or sunset. The warm light enhances flesh tones, creating a healthy glow. Scenes with heartwarming potential, such as a family get-together in the living room, are further enhanced by the warm orange glow produced by using daylight film indoors at night.

But what happens when you've been taking pictures indoors with tungsten-balanced film, and you move outside? Tungsten film exposed under daylight conditions produces cool, bluish tones. This is because the film is manufactured with a strong blue bias to compensate for the orange of tungsten lighting. The bluish rendition can create moods from tranquility to storminess. The blue cast of tungsten-balanced film can enhance foggy, misty scenes, or convey a feeling of extreme cold. Make sure your subject will be appropriate for this blue cast; red-toned subjects and flesh tones are usually unappealing.

One of the most interesting applications for tungsten film is in photographing cities at twilight. Blue tones in the afterglow

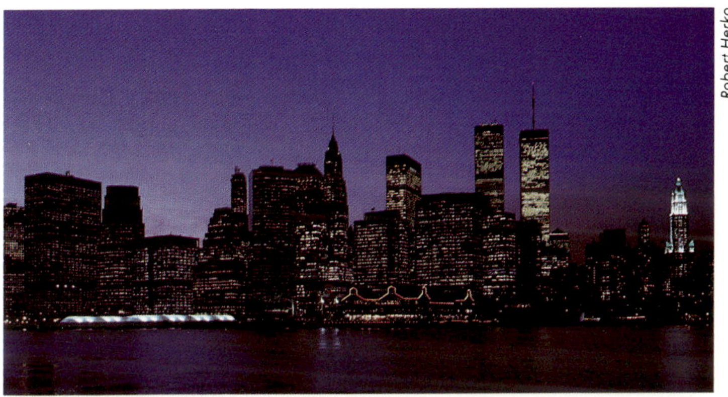

Robert Herko

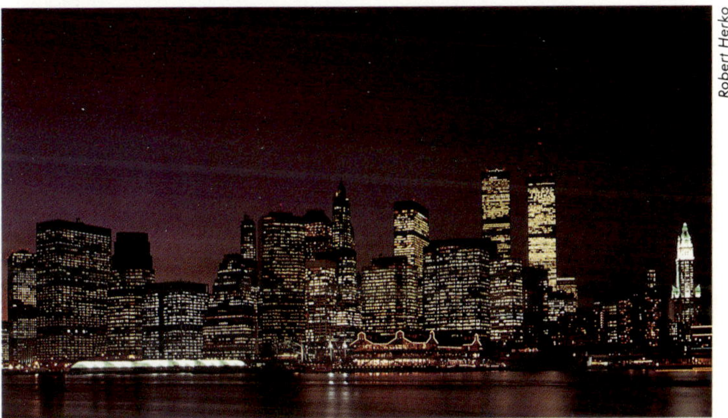

Robert Herko

In these photographs, daylight- and tungsten-balanced films were used to photograph the Manhattan skyline. Note the bluer, cooler tones of the photograph shot on tungsten film, and the more natural colors of the picture taken on daylight-balanced film.

of sunset are very intense, and the orange tones appear more neutral. Fluorescent lights appear blue-white, warm colors are subdued, and scenes have an overall monochromatic appeal.

However, when you photograph nearby subjects under fluorescent light, either daylight or tungsten film will give you eerily green results. This green cast can produce interesting effects if the subject matter is appropriate.

When you photograph under fluorescent illumination, use a shutter speed of 1/60 second or longer to avoid uneven expo-

KODAK Film	For use with*	Film Speed and Filter		
		Daylight	Tungsten Lamps (3200 K)	Photolamps (3400 K)
KODACHROME 25 (slide)	DEF	25 None	6 No. 80A	8 No. 80B
KODACHROME 64 (slide)	DEF	64 None	16 No. 80A	20 No. 80B
KODACHROME 200 (slide)	DEF	200 None	50 No. 80A	64 No. 80B
KODACHROME 40 (slide)	P	25 No. 85	32 No. 82A	40 None
EKTACHROME 100 HC (slide)	DEF	100 None	25 No. 80A	32 No. 80B
EKTACHROME 200 (slide)	DEF	200 None	50 No. 80A	64 No. 80B
EKTACHROME 400 (slide)	DEF	400 None	100 No. 80A	125 No. 80B
EKTACHROME 160 (slide)	T	100 No. 85B	160 None	125 No. 81A
KODACOLOR GOLD 100 (print)	DEF	100 None	25 No. 80A	32 No. 80B
KODACOLOR GOLD 200 (print)	DEF	200 None	50 No. 80A	64 No. 80B
KODACOLOR GOLD 400 (print)	DEF	400 None	100 No. 80A	125 No. 80B
KODACOLOR GOLD 1600 (print)	DEF	1600 None	400 No. 80A	500 No. 80B
EKTAR 25 (print)	DEF	25 None	6 No. 80A	8 No. 80B
EKTAR 125 (print)	DEF	125 None	32 No. 80A	40 No. 80B
EKTAR 1000 (print)	DEF	1000 None	250 No. 80A	320 No. 80B

*DEF—Balanced for daylight or electronic flash.
T—Balanced for tungsten lamps or existing tungsten light
P—Balanced for photolamps.

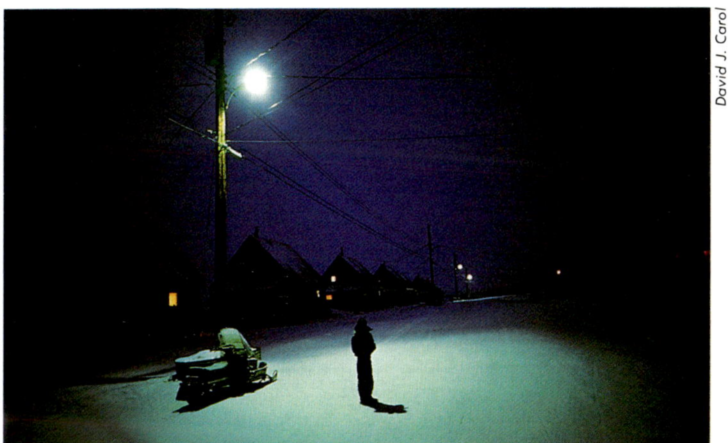

David J. Carol

Tungsten film used outdoors produces blue tones which can lead to unusual and graphic results.

sure caused by variations in brightness and color that occur during the alternating-current cycle of a fluorescent tube.

The chart on page 66 gives light-source, film-speed, and filter recommendations for Kodak color films.

Black-and-white film. Color film is so common today that you may think it's the standard. But many of the world's greatest photographers are known for their work in black and white. You may even have noticed a current trend toward black and white in advertising.

Why is this? Although color photographs are the most popular, many people are rediscovering the creative aspects of black-and-white reproduction. Black-and-white photos direct the viewer's attention to modeling, abstract forms and patterns, and textures.

One advantage of black-and-white films is the wide range of speeds they offer—from 25 to as high as 25,000 with push processing! At the low end of the speed range, films such as KODAK T-MAX 100 Professional and KODAK Technical Pan Films have extremely fine or micro-fine grain, which means that

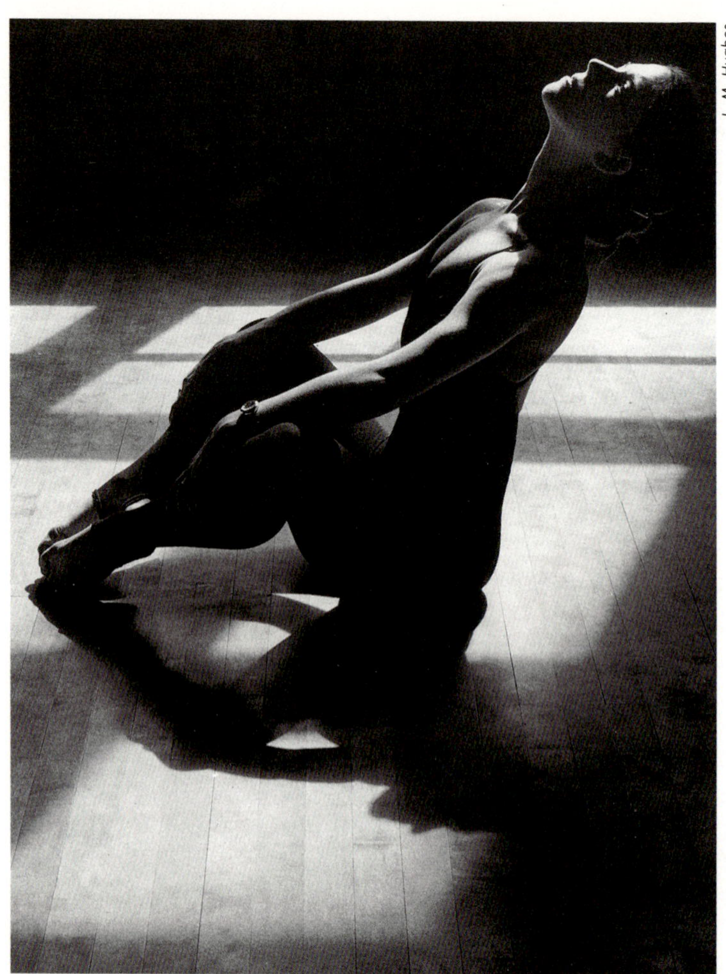

L. M. Hughes

Black-and-white photography emphasizes the compositional aspects of form and shape.

you can make very large high-quality prints from small negatives. With films at the high end of the range, such as KODAK T-MAX P3200 Professional Film, you can take photographs in extremely low light, stop fast action under low-light conditions, or handle long telephoto lenses without using a tripod.

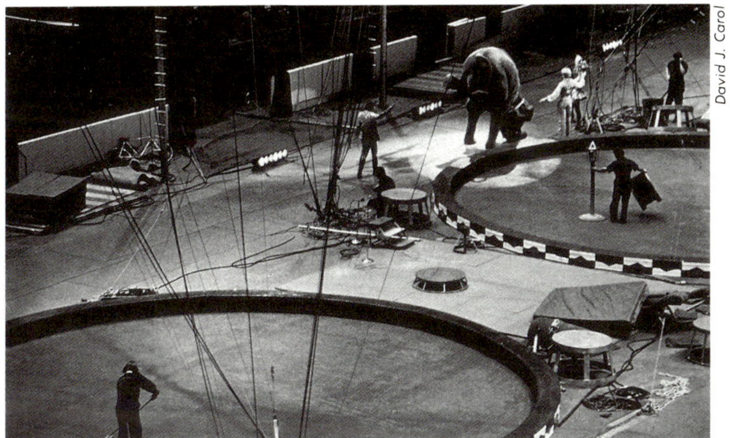

David J. Carol

Scenes that may look cluttered in a color photograph may be striking in black-and-white.

Panchromatic (sensitive to all colors) black-and-white films interpret the colors you see by reducing them to tones of black and gray. In some cases, the film will render two colors that look different to the eye—blue and green, for example—as almost the same shade of gray. But you can use a wide selection of filters to manipulate tone separation and produce many special effects.

A No. 25 red filter will darken a blue sky, and lighten skin tones; a No. 47 blue filter will do the opposite. A yellow filter, such as a No. 15 deep-yellow, will accentuate texture in brightly sunlit scenes by darkening shadow areas.

The chart on page 71 gives film speed, and descriptions of some popular Kodak black-and-white films.

Infrared film. Special-purpose films such as infrared black-and-white films are also available. Infrared films such as KODAK High Speed Infrared Film are sensitive to infrared radiation, and produce abstract tone reproduction. Often used for aerial, scientific, medical, and documentary photography, infrared film can also produce striking pictorial effects, such as eerie, dreamlike landscapes with light foliage and dark skies. It is also

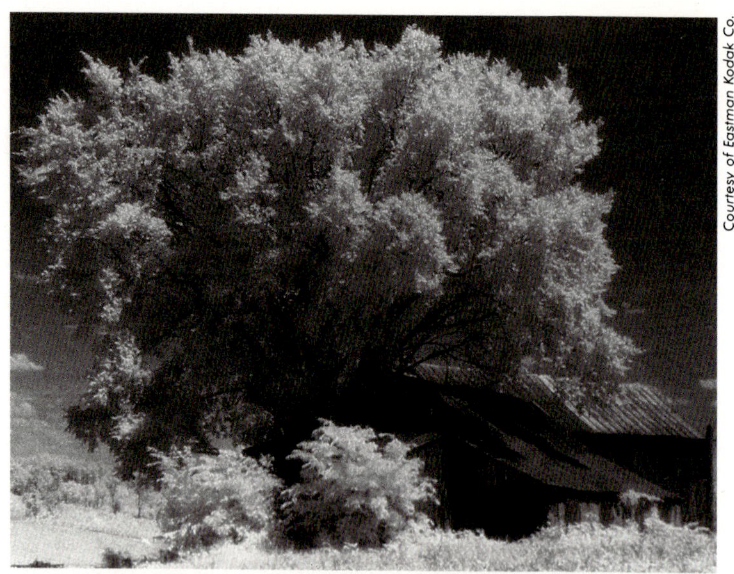

Courtesy of Eastman Kodak Co.

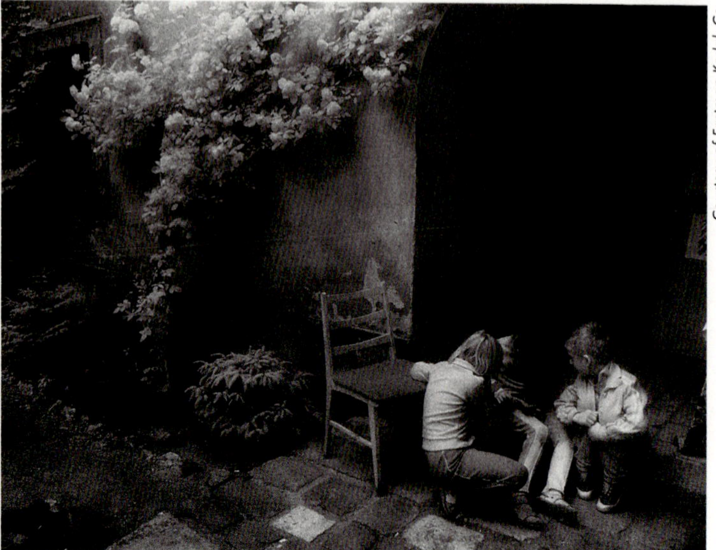

Courtesy of Eastman Kodak Co.

By recording light that is invisible to the human eye, infrared film produces eery and graphic portraits of ordinary objects.

Kodak Black-and-White Film	Description	Film Speed	Color Sensitivity
Continuous-Tone Film			
Technical Pan	Film with micro-fine grain for making extreme enlargements.	25*	Panchromatic, extended red
T-MAX 100 Professional	Medium speed for general outdoor photography; extremely fine grain.	100	Panchromatic
PLUS-X Pan	Medium-speed general-purpose film; extremely fine grain.	125	Panchromatic
T-MAX 400 Professional	High-speed film for dimly lighted subjects, good depth of field, or stopping action; extremely fine grain.	400	Panchromatic
TRI-X Pan	High-speed film for photographing action, existing light, use with telephoto lenses; fine grain.	400	Panchromatic
T-MAX P3200 Professional	Multi-speed film for very dim existing light, fast action, high shutter speeds combined with small lens openings.	1000†	Panchromatic
Special-Purpose Film			
High Speed Infrared	Infrared-sensitive for abstract effects in pictorial photography.	50 (Daylight)‡ 125 (Tungsten)‡	Infrared

* With processing in KODAK TECHNIDOL Liquid Developer

† Nominal speed with processing in KODAK T-MAX Developer. Has variable speed in a range from 800 to 25,000 with adjusted development times.

‡ With a No. 25 filter.

useful for showing detail ordinarily obscured by haze in distant landscapes.

To obtain infrared rendition in your photos, you must use a filter over the lens to absorb the blue and green light to which the film is sensitive. For general photography, use a No. 25 (red) filter. To record only infrared radiation, use a No. 89B, 88A, 87, or 87C filter.

Experiment with the many different types of black-and-white films to see what works best for you.

PUSHING FILM

Film is most often "pushed" to increase its effective speed for picture-taking under low-light conditions or stopping fast action. But pushing film can also be a creative technique to produce *enlarged grain*.

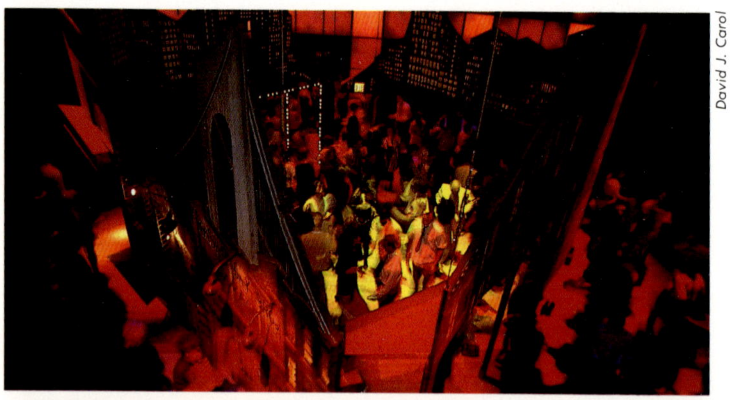

David J. Carol

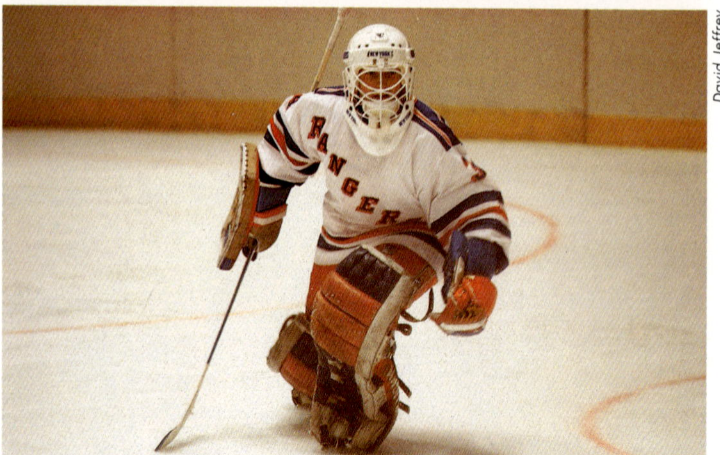

David Jeffrey

Underexposing and then push-processing film can help you in low-light or fast-action situations. The photograph at the top reveals the interior of the discoteque. In the lower photograph, action was frozen by using a fast shutter speed and then push-processing the film.

Color-slide and black-and-white films are the most commonly pushed films. By exposing the film at a higher speed and then extending the time in the first developer, you can push KODAK EKTACHROME Films. KODAK EKTACHROME P800/1600 Professional Film is a multi-speed film intended for pushing to a speed of 800, 1600, or 3200. You can push most pictorial black-and-white films by extending the development time.

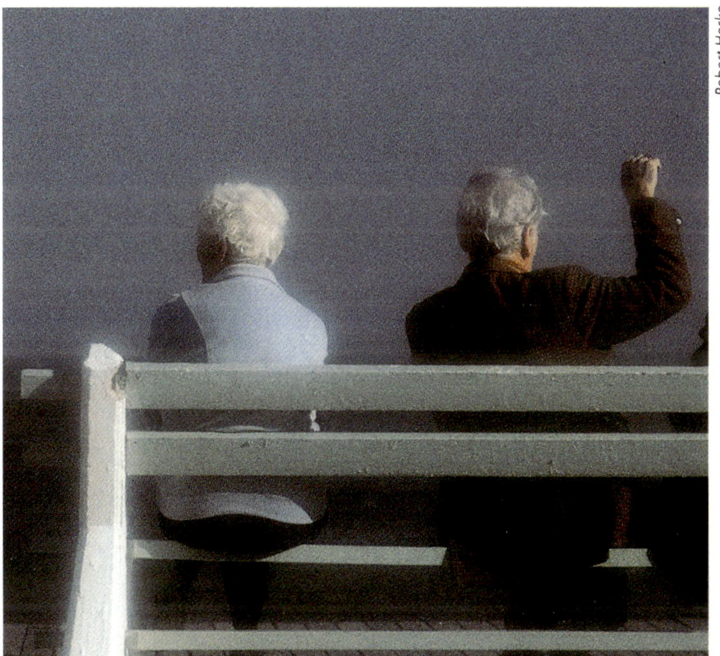

Robert Herko

Push-processing increases film graininess. This often heightens the graphic effect of the composition.

When you push high-speed films to even higher speeds, graininess becomes noticeable—especially when you enlarge the negative or slide image. Pushed and enlarged black-and-white images may take on the quality of a pencil or charcoal drawing. A color enlargement of grain more closely resembles an impressionist painting.

SANDWICHING SLIDES

A slide "sandwich" is created by following the same principles for composing a collage.

By sandwiching slides, you can create "impossible" combinations of subjects and backgrounds. You can add a setting sun, a moon, or just about any object to an existing scene.

Start by assembling images that show good potential for sandwiching. One of the easiest combinations consists of an image silhouetted against a pale or clear background sandwiched with a sunset, ocean, or blue-sky background.

The credibility of the slide sandwich depends on matching size, scale, lighting, and points of perspective in both images. Of course, nobody says all these elements must match exactly to be effective; mismatches will often produce surrealistic and dramatic effects.

Making a slide sandwich is actually quite simple. The key is to choose a slide that has clear or very light-colored areas that permit details from the second slide to show through. Using slightly overexposed slides will help show both images more clearly. Besides the two slides, you'll need some narrow transparent tape and a new slide mount to hold the slide sandwich together.

First remove the two pieces of film from the slide mounts. Remove dust from both sides of the film with compressed air; then place the films together to form the composition you want. Next, very carefully place tape along one of the sides of the sandwich that includes sprocket holes, and wrap the tape over the edge to hold the two films together. To make sure that the tape does not overlap the image area, use a very narrow strip. Leave the other edges untaped to allow for normal expansion and prevent buckling.

The final step is to mount the sandwich in a new cardboard or plastic mount. Carefully align the films with the guides in the new mount. Be careful not to scratch the film if you are using plastic mounts.

Sandwiching slides is like directing—you can order retake after retake by making different image combinations, as in these photographs of geese and a sunset.

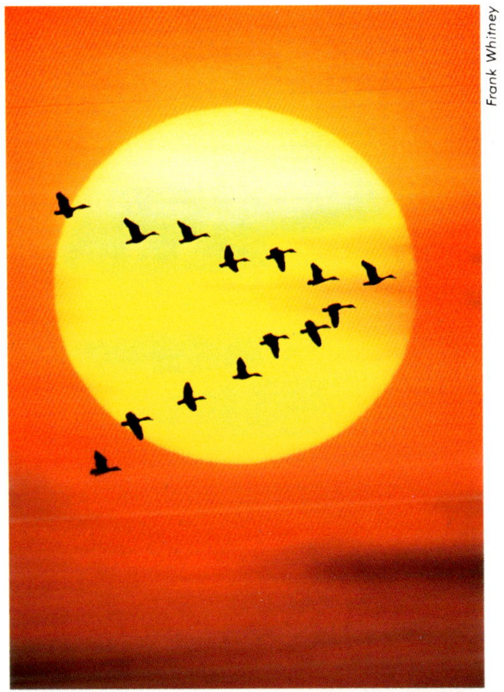

Frank Whitney

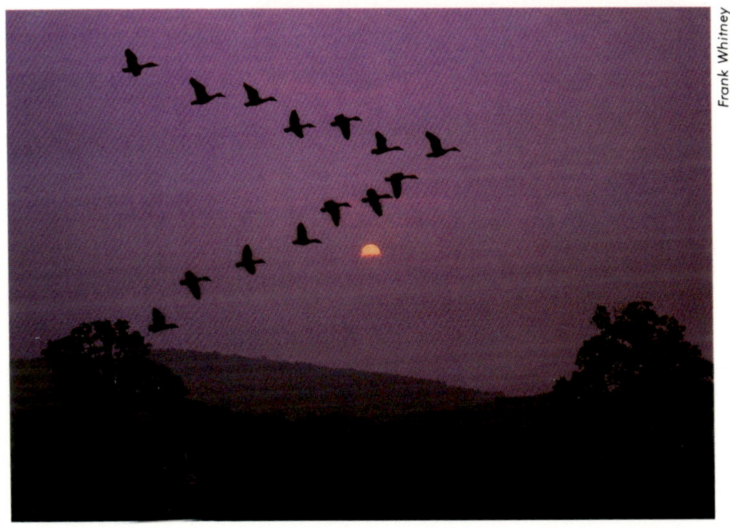

Frank Whitney

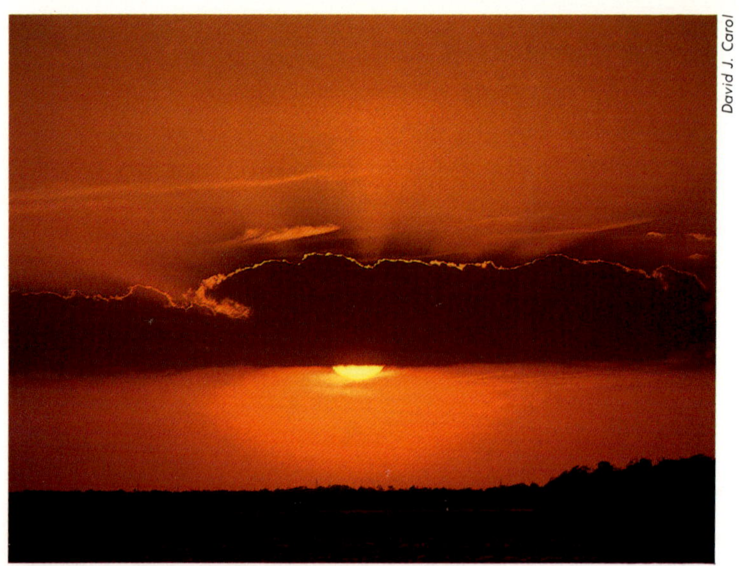

David J. Carol

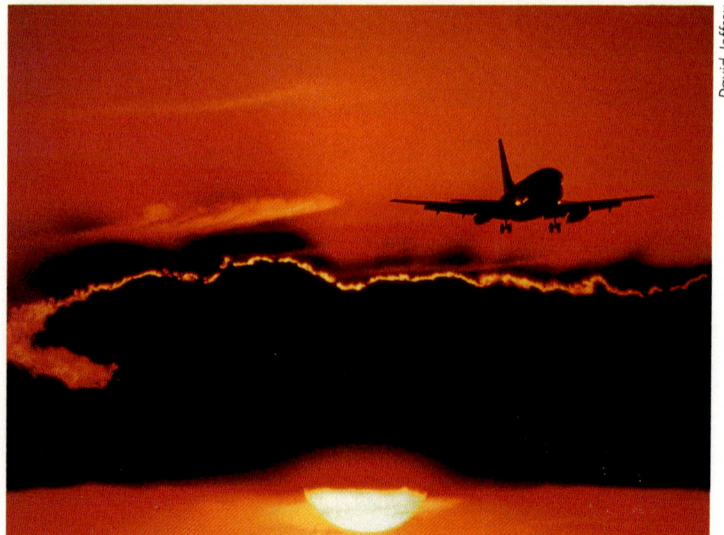

David Jeffrey

Not only can you alter reality when you sandwich slides, as shown by the plane placed against an enlarged sun, but you can also create "dreamscapes," as shown by the photo on the facing page.

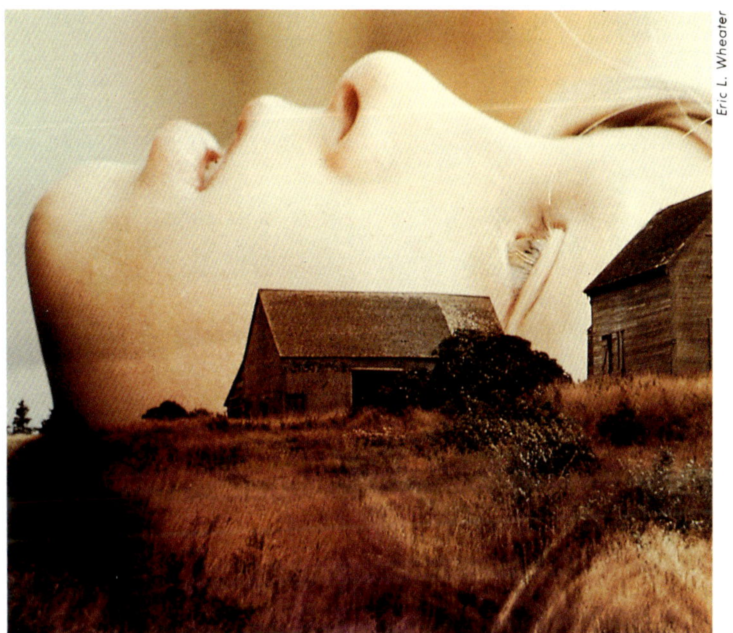

Eric L. Wheater

After you assemble your slide sandwich, you can project it with a standard slide projector for the enjoyment of your family and friends, or make color prints. You can also have slide duplicates made directly from the sandwich.

Don't feel that your sandwich images have to look realistic. The objective in sandwiching is to create visual excitement and expand your vision.

CONCLUSION. You must always learn the basics of a subject before you master the more advanced principles. This is certainly true of photography. A good grasp of composition, camera controls, exposure, and accessories ensures that you can meet the challenges as you strive for more creativity in your photography.

Once you've mastered the creative techniques outlined in this book, you'll be able to bend the rules to explore new photographic horizons.

GLOSSARY OF TERMS

Angle of view—The extent of the area "seen" by a lens.

Ant's-eye view—The point of view used to photograph an object from a low angle.

Aperture—Lens opening. The opening in a lens system through which light passes. The size is either fixed or adjustable. Lens openings are expressed as *f*-numbers.

Autofocus—Used to describe cameras that focus automatically on the subject when you aim the camera so that the subject is within the autofocus marks or brackets in the viewfinder.

Automatic flash unit—A flash unit with a sensor that measures the light reflected from a scene or the light at the film plane and shuts off when the proper amount of light has been emitted.

Bird's-eye view—The point of view used to photograph an object from above.

Bounce flash—A technique in which flash is directed at (or "bounced" off) a large reflective surface to provide softer, more diffused illumination.

Bracketing—Making extra photographs at exposure settings to provide more and less exposure than the calculated or recommended setting—for example, at +1, +2, −1, and −2 stops from the calculated setting.

Built-in flash unit—A non-detachable unit that is a part of some camera models. It is usually turned on by a button, but some units will automatically activate when the meter determines that the scene is too dark for proper exposure without flash.

Collage—A composition made of various materials glued on a picture surface.

Color compensating (CC) filter—A filter used to produce relatively small alterations in the color balance of a photograph to compensate for the color bias of a light source on the film itself.

Color temperature—A measurement of the color quality of light sources; expressed in degrees Kelvin (K).

Color *(of light)*—See **"Color temperature."**

Conversion filter—A filter used to balance film to a light source different from the source for which it is designed.

Crop marks—Marks made to indicate the part of an image that will be printed.

Daylight-balanced film—Film balanced to produce accurate color rendition in daylight or with electronic flash.

Dedicated flash—An advanced automatic flash unit designed to work with a specific brand or model of camera. It exchanges information with the camera to provide proper exposure.

Depth of field—The distance between the nearest and farthest objects in a scene that appear in acceptable focus in a photograph.

Diffraction filter—A filter inscribed with parallel grooves that break up white light to create prism-like effects in highlights.

Diffusion—Softening of detail in a photograph by using a diffusion filter or other material that scatters light.

Diffusion filter—A type of filter that diffuses light. Diffusion filters come in varying strengths: No.1 is the weakest; mist and fog filters are considerably stronger.

Direct flash—Flash that strikes the subject directly.

Dual-color filter—See **"Filter."**

Electronic flash—A brief but intense burst of light from the flashtube of a built-in or detachable flash unit; used to supplement existing light or provide the main light on the subject.

Enlarged grain—See **"Push-processing."**

Exposure—The amount of light that acts on a photographic material; a product of the intensity (controlled by the lens opening) and the duration (controlled by the shutter speed) of light striking the film.

Exposure meter—An instrument—either built into a camera or a separate, hand-held unit—that measures the intensity of light; used to determine the aperture and shutter speed for proper exposure.

Fill-in flash—Light from a flash unit that is used to brighten shadows created by the primary light source.

Film speed—The sensitivity of a film to light, indicated by an ISO number.

Film-speed setting—A camera setting—either manual or automatic—that tells the camera the speed of the film.

Filter—A piece of colored glass or other transparent material used over the lens to emphasize, eliminate, or change the color or density of the entire scene or certain elements in the scene.

Flash calculator dial—A control on a flash unit that tells the correct aperture for the camera-to-subject distance, or the correct distance range for a particular aperture.

Flash-synchronization (sync) shutter speed—The speed at which the shutter is synchronized with the firing of the flash.

Flashtube—The gas-filled tube of an electronic flash unit that emits a short, intense burst of artificial light.

***f*-number or *f*-stop**—A number used to indicate the size of the opening on most camera lenses. Common *f*-numbers are *f*/2, *f*/2.8, *f*/4, *f*/5.6, *f*/8, *f*/11, *f*/16, and *f*/22. The higher the *f*-number, the smaller the lens opening.

Focal length—The distance from the optical center of a lens to the film plane when the lens is focused at infinity.

Freezing action—A technique that makes an object in motion appear "stopped"; can be accomplished by using a high shutter speed or electronic flash.

Grain—A minute particle of silver or a cloud of dye in a photographic emulsion.

Hot shoe—A fitting on top of a camera that provides electrical contact between an electronic flash unit and the camera shutter for flash synchronization.

ISO speed—A system of the International Organization for Standardization for measuring film speed.

Lens—One or more pieces of optical glass or similar material that collects and focuses rays of light to form a sharp image on film.

Manual exposure control—A camera exposure system that allows the photographer to adjust aperture and shutter speed manually.

Manual flash—A flash unit that emits the same amount of light each time it fires.

Multiple exposure—Recording two or more images on the same frame of film.

Multiple-image filter—A filter with a faceted surface that creates multiple images of a single subject.

Night exposure—An exposure made at night that normally requires a wide aperture and a slow shutter speed or a time exposure.

Normal lens—A lens that produces an image with perspective similar to that of the original scene.

Off-camera flash—Using a flash unit off the camera to provide sidelighting, bounce lighting, or other directional lighting.

Overexposure—A situation in which too much light reaches the film, producing a dense negative or a light slide.

Panning—Moving the camera during exposure to follow a moving subject.

Point-and-shoot camera—An automatic non-SLR camera, usually with built-in flash.

Polarizing filter—A filter that blocks polarized light; used to darken a sky or eliminate reflections from nonmetallic surfaces.

Push-processing—Extending the development time for films that have been exposed at a film-speed rating higher than the normal rating; often produces a grainier image.

Rangefinder—A focusing device on non-SLR cameras. It shows the photographer two images of the subject that must be aligned for proper focus.

Reciprocity effect—The loss of effective film speed, change in contrast, or color shift that can occur when you use very long or short exposure times.

Red-eye—Caused by reflection of the flash by blood vessels in the back of the eye.

Reflector—Any device used to reflect light onto a subject.

Screw-mount filter—A filter with a threaded ring that screws directly into the lens barrel.

Selective focus—Using a large lens opening to produce a shallow depth of field to isolate a subject in sharp focus from a blurred background or foreground.

Shutter speed—The length of time that the camera shutter is open to expose the film.

Single-lens-reflex (SLR) camera—A camera that uses a prism and mirror to provide viewing through the picture-taking lens.

Skylight filter—The strongest type of ultraviolet (UV) filter.

Star filter—A filter with horizontal and vertical lines etched into its surface that makes specular light sources look like stars.

Stop(s)—Exposure increments. Each single-increment change in shutter speed or aperture represents one stop, and halves or doubles the amount of light striking the film. (Also see **"*f*-stop."**)

Sync (synchronization) cord—An extension cord that connects the camera to a flash unit to provide electrical contact and synchronization with the shutter.

Telephoto lens—A lens that creates a larger image of the subject than a normal lens at the same camera-to-subject distance.

Through-the-lens meter (TTL)—A built-in camera meter that determines exposure for the scene by reading the light that passes through the lens.

Time exposure—A comparatively long exposure with a duration of seconds, minutes or even hours.

Tripod—A three-legged camera support with a rotating hinged head to which the camera is attached.

Tungsten-balanced film—Film that has been balanced to produce accurate color rendition under tungsten light.

Tungsten light—Light from normal household lamps and ceiling fixtures (not fluorescent).

Ultraviolet (UV) filter—A filter used to cut through haze and eliminate the blue cast often seen in scenics or photographs made in open shade.

Underexposure—A condition in which too little light reaches the film, producing a thin negative or a dark slide.

Wide-angle lens—A lens that covers a wider field of view than a normal lens at the same subject distance.

Zoom lens—A variable-focal-length lens that can be used in place of a number of individual fixed-focal-length lenses.

Zooming—Increasing or decreasing the focal-length setting of a zoom lens to increase or decrease the subject image size.

INDEX

Please note: Entries which appear in bold refer to captions.

DEP. LEG. B-9.476-90